Plucked from a Mango Tree

An Indian Woman's Journey across the Ocean, through Cancer, and to Freedom

Anjuli Seth Nayak, M.D.

Open Water Books

Published by Open Water Books

P.O. Box 28404

Green Bay, WI 54324

© 2014 by Anjuli Seth Nayak, M.D. All rights reserved.

www.nayaksagainstleukemia.com

Book cover design and formatting services by BookCoverCafe.com

The content, design and views expressed or implied in this work are those of the author, not the publisher.

No part of this work may be reproduced, stored in a retrieval system, or transmitted in any way by any means—electronic, mechanical, photocopy, recording or otherwise—without prior permission of the author, except as provided for by USA copyright laws.

Scriptures taken from the Holy Bible, New International Version®, NIV®. Copyright © 1973, 1978, 1984, 2011 by Biblica, Inc.™ Used by permission of Zondervan. All rights reserved worldwide. www.zondervan.com The "NIV" and "New International Version" are trademarks registered in the United States Patent and Trademark Office by Biblica, Inc.™

ISBN:
978-0-9909715-0-4 (hbk)
978-0-9909715-1-1 (pbk)
978-0-9909715-2-8 (ebk)

Library of Congress Control Number: 2014955274

What others are saying about
Plucked from a Mango Tree

Anjuli Nayak's memoir will undoubtedly inspire cancer patients to look for spiritual resources within themselves and to undertake a personal spiritual journey to help them overcome their disease. She has unselfishly shared her personal story with us all and succeeded in inspiring us all. I respect and admire her not only as a very accomplished physician-researcher, a devoted mother and friend but also as a very brave woman who is taking a very difficult walk through life with great courage and dignity. Her book will give hope to all those undergoing cancer treatment for a new life after cancer.
Usha Raj, MD
Head, Department of Pediatrics
University of Illinois at Chicago
Chicago, IL

Dr. Anjuli Nayak's inspiring story highlights the hope that patients with acute leukemia now have, and the need for them to look beyond medical treatment. Today, doctors can do much about the disease, but more needs to be done to help patients re-build their lives, maybe different lives than before their cancers, but full and rich lives all the same. With this memoir, Dr. Nayak has truly given us a gift – a moving perspective on the vital role of treating the human spirit, and the wonders of cancer survivorship.
Michelle M. Le Beau, PhD
Arthur and Marian Edelstein Professor of Medicine
Director, Comprehensive Cancer Center
University of Chicago Medicine

I've followed Anjuli Nayak's journey with cancer very closely, as I've known her for many years as a talented researcher and wonderful mother. My years in drug research have shown me just what a tough battle fighting Acute Lymphoblastic Leukemia can be. Anyone with the disease, or is a caregiver to someone engaged in this battle, and be inspired and encouraged by Anjuli's story. Most of all, they can gain the hope that they, too, have a chance at victory in their own fight.

Daniel Levitt, MD, PhD

Table of Contents

Foreword	vii
Introduction and Acknowledgments	ix
Chapter 1: The Call That Changed My World	1
Chapter 2: The Games of India	3
Chapter 3: Early Memories	9
Chapter 4: The Trap of Tradition	17
Chapter 5: My Key to Freedom	25
Chapter 6: One More Step to Freedom	31
Chapter 7: The Study of Medicine	38
Chapter 8: Desires Granted; Hopes Destroyed	53
Chapter 9: Back in the Trap, but Not for Long	65
Chapter 10: A New Life Times Two	76
Chapter 11: Growing Pains	88
Chapter 12: Making Decisions in a Whirlwind	96
Chapter 13: Treatment Begins	102
Chapter 14: Poisonous Honey	111
Chapter 15: Dashed Hopes	124
Chapter 16: Exploring Options	136
Chapter 17: The Transplant	151
Chapter 18: Beginning to Hope	163
Chapter 19: Relapse	171
Chapter 20: The Journey Onward	179
Chapter 21: Surviving and Thriving	188
A Note from the Author	200

Foreword

I first became aware of Anjuli Nayak when she received the Clemens Von Pirquet Award from the American College of Allergy, Asthma, and Immunology at our annual meeting in 1987. Her abstract showing that certain deficiencies in immunoglobulin, either present from birth or acquired, may be cause of life-threatening infections in children fascinated me. I made it a point to meet this highly talented researcher.

Over the years I've taken great pleasure in mentoring Anjuli, and watched the success of her clinical and research practice with great interest. Her hard work and dedication to her patients brought relief to many, and contributed greatly to the body of knowledge used by allergists and immunologists world wide.

So it was with great sadness and distress that I learned of her illness, the deadly acute lymphoblastic leukemia. I encouraged her to put the same determination and drive that made her a successful physician into her fight against cancer. True to herself, Anjuli battled through the disease and came through victorious.

She is one of the fortunate ones, to be living in an era where cures for cancer are possible. Often I reminded her of this fact, and to not lose hope when her condition seemed to take a turn for the worse.

Many others will benefit from reading her memoir. Physicians can be reminded of what it's like to be on the other side of the chart, no knowing or understanding all that is going on.

Those fighting terminal illnesses can be encouraged, because of the advances in immunology and what we have learned in recent years. We are able to manipulate genes and treat diseases such as leukemia in ways that were simply not possible just a few years ago. This memoir can be a valuable source of inspiration to patients and their families, knowing possibilities for treatment and even cures are greater than ever before.

Joseph A. Bellanti, M.D.
Professor, Pediatrics and Microbiology-Immunology
Georgetown University School of Medicine

Introduction and Acknowledgments

For the last three years, I've been on a journey I never wanted to take. However, had I known at the outset where the journey was going to lead me, I still would have gone.

I'm speaking of my journey with cancer.

In late 2010, I was a busy, successful physician, happily married with three sons. The diagnosis of acute leukemia shredded my plans for the future and set me on a new course.

I thought that, as a doctor, I knew what I was getting into. That assumption was only partly true. I knew some of what was happening in my body from a medical point of view. What I didn't know was the emotional and spiritual havoc the disease would wreak upon me, or how my husband, also a physician, and sons (one a doctor, one in medical school, and the third finishing high school) would react and cope.

Partway through my treatment, I had a revelation: doctors treat cancer patients medically, and in doing so, often perform miracles. But that's only part of the treatment cancer patients need. What the doctors don't do to is teach those with cancer how to survive the disease, making a new life for themselves around the permanent changes the illness can leave behind. Even with all of my years in medicine, I had to learn how to create my own survivorship plan. (In fact, I had no idea I even needed one.)

As I learned about cancer survival and how to rebuild my own life, I was driven by the desire to help others through the same maze in which

I found myself. I wanted to point others to the multitude of survivorship resources available and encourage them to make use of them. If my story helps merely one person have a higher quality of life after cancer, my diagnosis and subsequent journey will have been worth it.

Part of my survival was coming to terms with my own limited lifespan. One of my sons encouraged me to write my memoir, partly so his children (should he ever have any) would know who their grandmother was.

As I pondered his suggestion, I realized there is much in my story that I hope will encourage and inspire others.

I began my life in India, born to Hindu parents. My early life reflects that culture as it was 50 years ago. The tale of those years is a story of the struggles which women in that culture faced and the triumph that could only be achieved through self-sufficiency and education.

With hard work and determination (and yes, stubbornness and strength of will), I left India behind and made a new life in the United States. The traits that made me successful in achieving my educational goals helped me advance in my career. I saw no reason to live unless I could be a success in these ways.

Until my diagnosis. Then the control I had always wanted over my life was stripped away. My story shifts to that of a nucleus being changed, a resurrection within and a path of discovery.

My journey, which started by my demanding my own will, took me to a place where I learned to embrace a greater love, peace, and belonging. I learned submission and surrender to a new birth, new paths, and new hopes.

And in the process, I realized my journey with cancer is just part of the journey of my life, that journey that God is taking me on. My journey with Him is unique and precious. I dream that every cancer survivor will experience this same journey, or rather, will experience his or her own unique journey with God.

My hope is that many will find inspiration in my story, that those with cancer can be encouraged by embracing the cancer and learning to accept a new and changed life. In acceptance, there can be great joy.

Those who are close to those with cancer may gain some insight into

INTRODUCTION AND ACKNOWLEDGMENTS

how their friend or family member may be feeling and know better how to understand what that person is experiencing.

As with any work, there are many to whom I am indebted. First, I am grateful to my parents, Mum-mee and Papa, who gave me the chance for an education whose value is unsurpassed.

My husband, Nick, and my children supported me on this journey, and I could not have survived without them. I couldn't be prouder than I am of you. Thank you for giving me strength and being pillars of support at every turn in my life.

Many thanks are due to the University of Chicago Comprehensive Cancer Center, which birthed me with a new life. I cannot speak highly enough of all of the doctors, nurses, and others who cared for me. If you have not been mentioned by name in this book, it does not mean I value your time, attention, and care any less. In gratitude for all I have received from the Cancer Center, all royalties from this book will be donated to the Center.

I am also grateful to the many people, especially my dear sisters in Christ, who prayed faithfully for me throughout my treatment.

Thanks are also due to my middle son, Zachary, for inspiring me to write my memoir. Without your prompting, I never would have undertaken this project.

This book would not completed without the support of my dear friend, Evelyn Puerto, whose life has always been a beacon of light and hope for me.

And lastly, thank You, God, for my past, present, and future, and for Your grace and mercy.

Chicago, IL
2014

Chapter 1
The Call That Changed My World

My fingers tightened around the cell phone as I sat in my car, my eyes widening, staring at nothing.

"Your white cell count is twenty-eight thousand with immature cells including blasts."

I could barely comprehend what the pathologist was telling me.

I set the phone in my lap and felt the words of my death sentence forming on my forehead: *acute lymphoblastic leukemia. How could this have happened?* I had been feeling a little tired the past few months, like I had been carrying around a heavy weight all day. As a physician, I knew that tiredness could be a symptom of a multitude of ills. That this fatigue was a sign of anything serious was as alien a thought as if I'd decided I no longer wanted to be a doctor. For months I'd blamed my fatigue on skipping workouts and the excitement of my oldest son's wedding. When I decided to get a routine blood test, I expected something like low thyroid—not a rare and aggressive form of cancer.

This day that had started so normally was whirling out of my control. My office was closed on Fridays, but my secretary would go in to take care of details and make sure there were no issues with patients who needed prompt attention. As usual, I called her at nine that morning to check on everything.

"Doctor," she told me, "an alert value on a blood test was faxed in last night." *Alert values* mean something is wrong with the test results, and generally I need to follow up with the patient right away. I sat up straighter.

"Go get it, please," I told her, "and tell me who it's for and what the results are."

I waited while she turned to the fax machine and heard the rustle of paper as she returned to the phone. "Doctor," she said hesitantly, "this test is for you." She paused. "Your white count is twenty-two thousand."

Immediately suspicious, as a normal count is around ten, I consulted my husband, who is also a physician. "You just have an infection, that's all," he said. I didn't think so, as my only symptom was fatigue—no fever or anything else to indicate infection.

Hoping it was a lab error, I called one of my nurses and asked her to stop by my home to draw another sample so the test could be repeated. She did so and hand-carried it to the lab, labeling it "stat." Trying to keep calm, I went for a massage. An hour of strong hands kneading my muscles couldn't break up the knot of worry inside me. As soon as I was done, I called the lab from my car and learned there had been no mistake.

I sat in my car wondering what would happen next. *How could this be happening?* One son had graduated from medical school and married, the second was in his last year of medical school, the third was a senior in high school. Our dreams for them were well on their way to fulfillment. My husband and I had a busy allergy practice, a comfortable life—everything we could possibly want.

God, I thought, *why are You doing this? I've done so much for others, looked after the widows and orphans, built a hospital in India. Now this.*

I leaned my head on the steering wheel. *Cancer. Leukemia.* Words I hadn't ever thought to associate with myself. What was God doing? I had fled one trap long ago. Now I found myself dangerously tangled in another one.

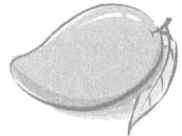

Chapter 2
The Games of India

Growing up in India, five o'clock was the high point of my day. I would pace back and forth, peering through the green glass panes of the front door, waiting eagerly for my father's return from the office. When he arrived, my mother, Krishna, would bring a cup of tea out to the veranda. Papa would settle into a worn rattan chair, and I'd watch him drink his tea. He was a good-looking gentleman, tall with skin so white he'd pass for an Englishman. When he finished drinking, we would get out the games—*Snakes and Ladders* or *Ludo*—or play card games like gin rummy with thirteen cards. For years we did this, from the time I was six to about fourteen or fifteen.

Sometimes my younger sister, Mridul, played with us. She wasn't as good at the games as I was. We let her play if she begged enough, giving in to her desire to please and the beautiful smile that rarely left her face.

My older siblings couldn't be bothered. My brother, Sudhir, was always busy with his own friends. Manju, my older sister, would say she had to study. As she got older, she'd spend her time making all kinds of concoctions to beautify herself. Some days she'd wash her hair in *ritha*, a fruit she'd mash up, seeds and all. She thought the ritha would make her hair grow longer and shinier, even though it smelled like rat's urine.

Then she'd sit for hours in the sun to dry her hair, letting the breeze lift the long, dark strands into a gravity-defying dance. Other times she would pour boiling water into a pan and lean over it with her head covered with a towel, letting the steam soak into her pores. Then she'd spend hours polishing her skin with a mixture of fresh cucumber juice and *malai*, the cream she'd skimmed from boiled milk. My mother approved of all of this activity. "Keep it up, Manju, you'll be sure to get a good husband."

My mother didn't have time for games. "Bhagwan," she'd say to my father, "you are wasting your time. What are you doing, sitting there playing games? Why don't you help those girls with their homework?"

Papa would roll his eyes and put some tobacco in his mouth and chew it. He thought it calmed his mind and took the sting out of my mother's nagging, which was as persistent as hungry mosquitoes. While he was at work, my mother would search all of the drawers, feeling under all his clothes, looking for his supply of tobacco so she could throw it out. She never did find it all, but she knew his favorite hiding places. Usually she managed to unearth most of it.

Confiscating Papa's tobacco was one of my mother's confusing inconsistencies. On the first of the month, she would wait with me for my father to come home—more impatient than I was. When he arrived, she'd hold out her hand without saying a word. Papa would turn his wages over to her. She would count the rupees and give him twenty, his monthly allowance for tobacco. Why she gave him the money and then took the tobacco he bought with it never made sense to me.

Mum-mee never trusted the household help, thinking that as they were very poor, they would steal cash or jewelry. She was compulsive about keeping everything locked in the safe or in metal cabinets, and she kept the keys tied to her waist under her sari. I would wait for her to leave the keys on her dressing table, which she only did when she was taking a bath, seizing my chance to pilfer them and take a look at what she had locked up. Usually I found a few rupees along with the jewelry. I never took anything; I was simply indulging my child's curiosity to know what was there.

CHAPTER 2: The Games of India

Our house was like a train station with people's coming and going. Relatives—aunts, uncles, cousins, grandparents—constantly visited. While we enjoyed these visits, my father's stepmother was not my mother's favorite visitor. When Daddi-ji came to call, she would hunt for my mother. Usually they'd meet in the kitchen. She would push my mother away from the stove or sink. "You don't know how to cook; you are doing it all wrong."

Daddi-ji was strict about keeping the kitchen clean, pure, and holy, what was called *achutth*. If you entered the kitchen without taking a bath, while wearing slippers, or while menstruating, you had defiled the room, making it *chutth*, or "unclean." Cooking onions, garlic, or meat were also taboo. Daddi-ji routinely took over the food preparation in our home, keeping up a constant stream of abuse. "You are polluting your house, you know, letting those cats and dogs into it. What else could I expect from a woman who feeds her family eggs or onions?" She would shake her head. "At least you don't try to give them meat."

My mother would argue back. "Your son likes the eggs and the onions. Don't you know that?"

Daddi-ji would take up the fight with my father. "Bhagwan, you have a horrible wife. Do you hear the way she talks to me? Everything in her kitchen is polluted. She can't do anything right; she's so incompetent. She's defiling you all with unholy foods." Out of respect for her, my father would tell my mother to do as Daddi-ji said.

Even as a child, I knew Daddi-ji was wrong. She was like the pig that only sees the mud in the pond and ignores the flowers on the bank. All she noticed were what she considered my mother's defects, and she had no eyes for her strengths.

That my mother loved her children, I was sure of, and she tirelessly cared for us. Daddi-ji's insults were tiny needles that stabbed my soul, even though I knew they were unfair. I wondered if all mothers-in-law were like her, wanting to find fault, persecute, and ostracize the women their sons had married. Having a cruel or critical mother-in-law would be like playing a game with an opponent you could never beat.

Father would chew more tobacco and try to make peace. His stepmother's influence over him waned after she nearly killed my brother,

5

Sudhir. She refused to allow my parents to vaccinate him for smallpox. When he contracted hemorrhagic smallpox and almost died, only the intervention of my mother's physician brother saved Sudhir's life. He was able to get the right treatment. My mother finally was able to overrule her mother-in-law and get my sisters and me vaccinated.

Gentle as he was, my father did take up for me. We always celebrated my brother's birthday because he was a boy. Mum-mee didn't think it was necessary to celebrate for girls, and besides, in her mind, recognizing birthdays was an American custom—not an Indian one. I wanted to mark my birthday in some way, so I put up a fuss. My father agreed that I was right, and from then on, we celebrated everyone's birthdays.

We had little money for restaurant meals. But starting around my tenth year, we celebrated my birthday and my brother's at the Chinese restaurant called Chung Fa. (Now that I think about it, I can't remember what we did for my sisters' birthdays.) There was a large Chinese community in our town, established generations ago. Most of these Chinese immigrants were either dentists or owned food places. Chung Fa was the only air-conditioned restaurant around, equipped with small rattling window units insufficient to dilute the smell of all the Chinese spices—the savory ginger, garlic, and sesame—trapped inside.

Our family of six would crowd into one of the twelve booths. I always ordered the chicken corn soup and vegetable chow mein. As Hindus, we were vegetarians, so it was a real treat to have chicken. Then we'd go to the market and purchase vanilla pastries with vanilla ice cream.

Maybe I was so insistent about celebrating because birthdays were special days in the convent school I attended. Normally we had to wear uniforms, but not on our birthdays. Like all of the other girls, as my birthday approached, I would plan my outfit carefully, wanting to outdo what all of the others wore on their birthdays. One year I picked my sky-blue dress with roses on it; another, the pink taffeta with a lace underskirt. I still remember every birthday dress I wore all of the years I attended that school. Candy, usually forbidden, was allowed on birthdays. The birthday girl would bring in pieces of hard candy and place two on each desk, and she would give some to the teachers. The whole class would stand and sing "Happy Birthday" in English, with some additional verses:

May God bless you, we pray,
May God bless you, we pray,
May God bless you, dear Anjuli,
May God bless you, we pray.
Happy long life to you,
Happy long life to you,
Happy long life, dear Anjuli,
Happy long life to you!

I was happy living with my family, but even then, I didn't want a long life in India. Starting from the third grade, every Friday in school we watched documentary films released by UNICEF. Most of them were about the lives people lived in America. I saw boys and girls playing together, smiling and laughing, singing songs, and playing sports. Around that time, I also read a series of books by Enid Blyton, an English author who wrote about families sending their children—even the girls—to boarding schools. How I yearned to have freedom like the girls in America and England—the freedom about which I had learned from the movies and the books! I saw equality, togetherness, and teamwork between boys and girls, something that was impossible even to dream of in India.

Why was it impossible? In India, girls were of no account. Boys carried on the legacy of the family. When girls marry, they no longer belong to the family of their birth. They become members of their husband's family. To the birth family, every daughter is a liability—someone they have to marry off so someone else will have to support them. Women were not viewed as producers in society, so they were regarded as having little or no value.

As a result, boys ruled the house, and ours was no different. My brother did whatever he wanted: smoked, drank, yelled, screamed—anything girls were not allowed to do. Boys always had pocket money, girls had none. I never learned to swim or to ride a bike; both were forbidden activities for girls. We accepted this inequity as a part of the way it was. We never liked it; we simply knew there was no point in even asking for anything different. It's no wonder my cute baby sister always dressed in boy's clothing when she was small. Even then she understood that being a boy had privileges.

As a young girl, I realized India was a trap for women—a trap that I desperately wanted to escape. The only time I bucked the culture was to press for an education, which I knew was the key that would set me free. An education was only hope of leaving behind India and the way the nation oppressed women.

I was blessed to have been born in a more modern time when the upper castes were beginning to educate their daughters. I thought about other girls who didn't receive a premium education like I did. Their lives had value, but they were treated like cattle. My first cousin was hard of hearing because of a childhood illness, but no one would buy her hearing aids. After all, why invest in a girl no one will want to marry?

The movies and books revealed what life could be like for me, a life with freedom and equality. I knew I would have to work hard to create that life for myself. What I didn't know at that young age was how much toil and pain my ambition would cost me.

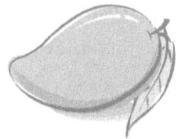

Chapter 3
Early Memories

In the year that the world convulsed with the death of Stalin and the coronation of Queen Elizabeth, when the structure of DNA was discovered and the polio vaccine developed, I was born in September of 1953. My earliest memories are of playing in a beautiful garden filled with poppies, dahlias, snapdragons, roses, jasmine, and gardenias—a vibrant mix of red, yellow, orange, violet, and pink flowers that perfumed the air with sweet and subtle fragrances. Even today, when I smell the same scents, the memory of that garden bursts into my mind. The gardener, a shepherd, cared for me and pulled the weeds from the garden. He said the weeds didn't need to be around the pretty flowers.

During my early years, we moved around from one place to another. My father worked for the state government, and he was transferred often. His job was to promote the development of manufacturing and industry in the district. He would travel to different towns, granting permits, sending people to do inspections, overseeing fiscal policies, and regulating franchises.

When the British ruled India, they did not have much interest in developing the nation's industry. In their view, India was merely a cheap source of raw materials. The British did construct a few cotton and jute mills, but little else. Following independence in 1947, India had to import many things to make industry possible, even steel, iron, and machinery. The Indian government began promoting industrial development as a way to produce manufactured goods as well as to provide a means of creating better-paying jobs for the poor, much like the Industrial Revolution that occurred in the United States nearly a century earlier.

As many people wanted to become entrepreneurs, my father kept busy helping them get their businesses approved and their industries established and producing. The government offered some small business startup loans, which my father, as the government's agent, would grant based on his trust in the applicants.

His business connections proved valuable to us all, providing an escape from the withering summer heat and the dust storms that raced over the thirsty north Indian plains. One man had a cottage in the hill station in Mussoori, which he lent to my father for the hottest three months of the year—the steamy summer when the temperature rarely fell below 100°. He also provided a jeep to take us there. Granting us this respite was his way of thanking my father for his assistance.

While we were glad to get away, traveling fourteen hours with seven people in a jeep with no air conditioning was no fun. My parents sat on the front seat; the hired man, my siblings, and I crammed into the seats that ran along the sides of the jeep. The area in between was packed with luggage, making one big bed. We took the trip in two days, traveling the first day to the foot of the hills, where we spent the night with friends. The next morning, we would tackle the ascent, winding back and forth on unpaved roads, climbing the Himalayas up to an elevation of seven thousand feet.

My father didn't want to tax the borrowed jeep, so he had to stop frequently to give it a rest. Orchards lined the roads, so when he parked the jeep in a shady spot, we children took the opportunity to pick whatever was growing. Trips fell into a rhythm: we stop at one place and pick apples. We pile in the back of the jeep. Papa starts driving on the winding, bumpy road. Five minutes later we all throw up apples. Then

CHAPTER 3: Early Memories

we stop again. At this stop we might find almonds or cashews. Five minutes later, we throw up the nuts.

The road continued like this for thirty miles; all of us children were hungry and thirsty but not able to keep anything down due to the rocking, twisting motion of the jeep. As we got closer to the top of Camel Back Hill, my mother would try to encourage us. "Hold on," she'd say, "only a few more miles." Her words didn't always work.

The cottage had many bedrooms but no electricity or running water, and as it was high in the hills, we found it very cold. While the temperature during the days hovered in the seventies, during the nights it could sink under fifty. The hired help would prepare the *braziers*, little clay pots that burned wood and coal. Small grills sat on top of these pots so people could cook on them. When the cooking was done, the braziers were placed around the room for heat.

As children, we loved the life at the hill station. We enjoyed the clean breezes, so different from the dusty air of the lowlands. We only had to take baths on Sundays, as all the water came from the well. My mother thought that since it was so cold, we weren't getting dirty.

Every day we would get up, eat milk, eggs, and toast for breakfast, and bundle up so we'd be warm enough to sit and read. At noon we'd walk three miles to the open-air market. Our route took us past a thick forest that surrounded a cemetery, a place that scared me when I was a child because I was told that ghosts lived there. When the wind rustled the leaves, I was convinced the spirits of those who had died were coming to hover over their graves. While I never saw any, I was sure they would look like shadowy bats and owls, gleaming white.

Once in the town square, we would spend the afternoon and evening there, meeting friends from different towns who were also spending their summers in the hills, wandering the market, a never-ending source of amusement. Vendors who sold their wares from four-wheeled carts crammed its narrow lanes. Many sold roasted rice or roasted *gram*, a seed shaped like a garbanzo bean. The market was filled with the aroma of roasting grains and the popping noise the kernels made as they were thrown into the furnace, making a kind of popcorn.

Other vendors sold pressed and dried mango and a concoction made out of tamarind fruit, black salt, mango powder, and sugar. We called it *churan,* and I loved it. I was told this churan was a good digestive element for your stomach. It was like the Sour Patch candy American kids eat, sweet and tart and chewy.

Still other stands were filled with balloons attached to a skeleton of bamboo. These balloons, round or long or shaped like a glove, came in all colors. Other vendors sold handmade and hand-carved toys of bamboo, such as whistles that made alarming sounds. We loved to scare each other with them. When we'd had our fill of the market, we'd head over to the Regal Theatre to see an American movie like *The Sound of Music.*

Another favorite of mine was the ice cream man, who pushed a refrigerator on three wheels up and down the aisles of the market, calling to people, playing a melody over and over to attract children. Years later, when I came to America and heard the ice cream truck for the first time, I was enchanted to hear the same tune I had followed as a child. For whatever reason, till this day, hearing that melody prompts my feet to hurry to the nearest place to purchase a vanilla ice cream bar wrapped in chocolate.

We usually remained in the mountains two, maybe three months, at least for all of May and June. My father stayed most of the time, sometimes leaving for a while in the middle to go back to work. Still, he was able to spend most of the hot weather in the cool of the hills before we all returned home to wherever we were living at the time.

When I was about ten, we returned to Kanpur, where I was born. Kanpur at that time was the largest industrial town in the state of Uttar Pradesh, which lies on the northern plains of India. Known as the "Leather City," its factories made harnesses and saddles for the Indian Army. Its mills produced khaki cloth. The smell of wet leather hung over the city like a foul-smelling cloud. No one wanted to go to that side of the city because of the stench.

The city itself hugged the right bank of the Ganges River, which was of great importance to Hindus all over India. The river originates

CHAPTER 3: Early Memories

from a glacier in the Himalayas, so everybody believed that the water was clear, pure, and holy. Bathing in the water was considered an important ritual for washing away sins. Houses, temples, and apartment buildings crowded the shore. Wide stone steps led down to the river to allow the faithful to perform ritual bathing in the Ganges, using the water for purification and other ceremonies.

Like many others, my grandmother went to the river daily. At four in the morning, Daddi-ji would take off her shoes and walk to the Ganges to bathe. She would take a small container with her to bring home some of the holy water. On the way back, she'd gather flowers. At home she would bathe her idols in the holy water, dress them up, and give them the flowers. She did all this believing these rituals washed away her sins.

We considered ourselves favored to live near the banks of the holy river. Relatives who lived in other towns would come to visit just for the chance to bathe in the holy river, so we had an unusual amount of company.

Unfortunately for us, when we first moved back to Kanpur, no government-provided housing was available. We had to set up temporary quarters in the annex of a factory. An armed guard patrolled around the clock, as the area was unsafe. We all slept on a concrete patio, each of us on a hemp bed. One night my mother heard something hit the window, and footsteps sounded on the loose gravel that surrounded the patio. She sat up and screamed, "Thief! Thief! Get him!"

Thieves! From an early age, ever since I started watching movies with my parents, I became acquainted with stories of thieves and *dacoits*. Thieves came to steal with homemade knives, while dacoits came in gangs on horseback and abducted women, taking them into the dense forest to be their slaves. Now I was awakened by my mother's screams, and I realized one of my deepest fears was about to become a reality.

The guard shot a few times in the air. We saw two men, naked except for loincloths, their bodies shining in the moonlight, slick from the oil they'd smeared on their skin to make it harder for anyone to grab them. They climbed the roof and disappeared.

Later, the guard escorted me to the bathroom in the back, lighting the way with his torch. When we opened the door, we saw a loincloth-clad man with a dagger at his waist clinging to the wall. My heart plummeted. I felt as unable to move as if I had turned to concrete, all except my chattering teeth. As always, when I am excited or frightened, the hair on my arms and the back of my neck stood up. We had all heard the stories of hyenas stealing children and thieves who came to rob and destroy; now I was living out my worst fears.

The guard pushed me aside and kept the man trapped in the bathroom until the police came to take him away. I clung to my mother's chest, shaking and trembling. There was no sleep for me that night or for many days after.

After several months of living in the annex, we settled into a one-story house that was about 150 years old. The cement walls were painted yellow, and cracks climbed up them like vines. Pale orange trim framed the flat roof. The front door was arched and had green glass panes in the upper half, one of which was broken. We never had the money to fix it. When I was in my late fifties, I returned for a visit. That same pane was still broken. I never felt safe in that house; the locks didn't work well, and we always had at least one broken window. Every night I prayed hard to be able to fall asleep so I could wake in the morning and find myself alive and well, untouched by intruders.

Visitors came in the front door right into the drawing room. Unlike the rest of the house, this room was painted white, and a carpet covered the floor. The rest of the seven rooms were pale blue. Dirty brown smudges crawled up the lower part of all the walls. To discourage robbers, none of the rooms had large windows, only small ones near the ceiling. The kitchen was equipped with a small gas stove, a faucet for washing dishes, and some shelves. We only had one bathroom, consisting of one alcove with a squatty potty and another for bathing. The bathing alcove was a small, square-tiled area with a drain and a tap. We'd fill the bucket from the tap and use a small round container called a *lotta* to pour water over ourselves. A sink for hand washing stood on spindly metal legs on the veranda. No doors connected the rooms, only arches.

CHAPTER 3: Early Memories

We kept our gods in a sacred area, a small room dedicated to the idols we worshiped. These idols were either copper statues, usually four or five inches in height, or small painted pictures. A small bell stood near the idols, ready to be rung at the start of worship. Like most Hindus, we worshiped different gods for different reasons, and we celebrated festivals commemorating the exploits of these gods. We worshiped Ram and Krishna, of course, along with Ganesh, Shankar, and Hanuman, who looked like a monkey and helped the god Rama in countless adventures against the Demon King. We also worshiped goddesses: Parvati, who was benevolent but could be wrathful in some incarnations, and Lakshmi, the goddess of good fortune, wealth, and well-being.

All of these gods and goddesses had fasts and festivals like Diwali, the Festival of Lights, and Holi, the Festival of Color. Our extended family would gather for feasting and worship of the idols. My childhood was filled with these family get-togethers, either at our house or at a relative's.

Sometimes we children participated in the ceremonies. All girls and boys went through a ceremony called *mundan* sometime during their first six or seven years of life. During this ceremony, the child's head is shaved as a purification ritual. It is believed that the hair a child is born with carries undesirable traits from past lives. The shaving symbolizes freedom from those past lives, enabling the child to move into the future.

I did my mundan with my sister Mridul on the same day our brother performed his thread ceremony, an initiation ritual limited to boys. The thread ceremony symbolizes the transferring of spiritual knowledge to the next generation of males. During the ritual, my brother was given a secret thread, which symbolizes his debts to teachers, parents, and scholars, who have given him wisdom and knowledge, and authorizes him to perform certain sacred rituals. Of course the thread ceremony was much more important than we girls and our mundan, so all of the attention focused on Sudhir. My father and brother celebrated the thread ceremony in the morning with all the pomp and show my parents could arrange. Later, in the afternoon, after we'd eaten and most of the relatives were still there, they did our mundan.

Neither my sister Mridul not I were surprised that our brother received more in the way of gifts. If we received ten rupees, he got fifty. The size of a gift was how people indicated which life events they thought were important. Still, Mridul and I got to wear our best clothes and eat some of our favorite treats: *purri*, deep-fried tortillas; *ladu*, balls of sugar and honey; and *barfi*, made from ground cashews, almonds, and honey. So we were happy.

I still remember one of my gifts: a storybook with pictures of animals that made noises when they were pressed. That book is more vivid in my mind than the ceremony, which I did not understand at all, since the pundit spoke mostly in Sanskrit. From time to time he would give directions to us in Hindi using a singsong voice: "Now you put some floo-ow-ers in front the statue, now you put some foo-ood, now you put some ri-ice." I had no idea of the significance of any of these ceremonies.

After the mundan, I had to wear a scarf on my head until my hair grew back. Although my head roasted under the summer sun, I wore the scarf even when I went to my dancing lessons. The teacher didn't mind during practice, but for the performance, he wanted me to remove it. "Let the people see your hair," he said.

"There is no hair," I replied, pushing back the scarf.

His eyes grew wide, and his jaw dropped when he saw my bald head. Still, to my great embarrassment, he made me perform without the scarf.

While I didn't understand much about Indian traditions at the time, I knew I didn't like being constrained by them. These were the earliest glimmers of a rebellion that would eventually define the direction of my life.

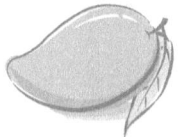

Chapter 4
The Trap of Tradition

Our house in Kanpur sat on six acres and was surrounded by banyan trees that stood like guards, their aerial roots making each tree look like several had melded together. My father fixed a swing with hemp ropes so we could swing from the trees. Living among all those trees were lizards, chameleons, and poisonous vipers, so I didn't feel too safe in the yard. Our house had a mosaic floor that kept cool in the summer. Twice we discovered vipers under the bed, seeking relief in the dim coolness. I was petrified for my life. Everybody had to leave the house so the gardener and housekeeper could beat the gray snakes around the head with bamboo sticks until they were sure they were dead.

Mixed among the banyan trees were those that bore fruit: lemons, limes, papayas, bananas, and tall mango trees, with their rounded canopies and long, thin leaves. Filling much of the yard were the vegetables my mother tended. For many years, money in our family was scarce as water in the dry season, so my mother raised food for the family: potatoes, onions, rice, beans, soya, lentils, eggplant, okra, tomatoes, cabbage, green beans, and greens. About the only food staple we bought was sugar.

In the years following independence, the government issued ration cards, but fearing a famine, the grocers hoarded food. To protect her family, my mother decided to grow everything herself. I remember helping her with this work sometimes, understanding that good food was unaffordable and that growing our own fruits and vegetables provided healthy food in abundance.

My mother was short, heavyset, and always in motion. She devoted herself to caring for her four children. As we grew older, growing food was a way for my mother to save for our education. She skimped and saved, cutting out alcohol and tobacco except for my father's chewing tobacco, which was the cheapest vice available. Somehow she also found time to grow roses, carnations, dahlias, pansies, petunias, snapdragons, and ornamental greens. I liked to dry pansies between sheets of newspaper and make cards out of them.

My mother had more practical uses for the flowers. She used the dried rose petals to flavor desserts such as sweet rice. She also set up a table in the street and sold the dried rose petals. Then she branched out. We kept two cows, and we couldn't possibly drink all of the milk as they could produce as much as 40 liters a day. Mum-mee started selling the extra milk. When produce was in season, we would eat as much as we could. Mum-mee sold the rest. For some reason, every year we were buried under an abundance of green beans and squash, and we would eat nothing else for weeks. To this day I can't even think about eating a green bean.

After I started attending the convent school at about the age of eight, I found my mother's commercial activities humiliating. Afternoons, I would get off of the bus, and there she would be, hawking her onions and milk. My classmates were all from rich families, so none of their parents had to think about ways to get extra money.

On our property stood small blue outbuildings where the gardener, the sweeper, and their families lived. This gardener was not anything like the nurturing gardener from my early memories. As a child I wondered why my mother was always so protective, making sure my sisters and I were never alone with this man. As I grew older, I found out. Like many men of his caste, he routinely groped girls of any age. Mother was constantly on guard to protect us from the gardener or any other male household help, making sure she "maintained the segregation of

CHAPTER 4: The Trap of Tradition

men and womenfolk," as she put it. She knew the males would take any opportunity to fondle the young girls when she wasn't around.

What she didn't know was the behavior of a friend of the family. When this man visited, he would put his hand in his underwear and ask me to press on it or to hold my hand on top of his. As much as I detested complying, I didn't feel I had a choice, and I knew I could never tell my mother. Anything to do with sex was a taboo subject for women, never to be discussed.

Seeing how the gardener and the sweeper lived gave me a close look into the caste system of India, which is the longest-lived system of slavery the world has known. At the top are the Brahmins, who take care of the temples and the spiritual needs of the people. Next is the caste of warriors and rulers, the Kshatryia, the caste into which I was born. Over time, this caste took on administration, defense, and maintaining law and order. My father, as a government official, worked in a position traditional to our caste.

Below the Kshatryia are the Vaishya, the businessmen and traders. Still lower are the Shudras, who do the skilled and unskilled labor, like gardening. At the bottom are the Dalits, the untouchables, those who perform the most menial tasks.

Caste is determined at birth; born a Brahmin or an untouchable is how one will die. For the Shudras and Dalits, all that waited was a life of destitution and desperation, the same burden that generations before them bore with no hope of redemption.

Our gardener, a Shudra, tended to the cows and the vegetables. The Dalits who lived behind our house swept and cleaned the toilets. To avoid polluting our house when they came into it, they had to shout when they arrived. Someone from the family would open the door for them and push back the curtains. If the Dalit touched anything, the house would be contaminated. When they left, one of us girls would have to mop the floor where they had walked to remove any pollution left behind.

In compensation for their work, the Shudras and Dalits received housing, food from the garden, hand-me-down clothing, and furniture and household items we no longer wanted.

Domestic violence was common in India, especially among the lower castes. Men of these castes had little value in society, and the women had even less. Females were more or less thought of as property to be treated as the owner wished. Regularly, the father of the Dalit family behind us would get drunk and beat his wife. She'd scream; the children would wail. Every year she gave birth to a child. If the baby was a girl, she was viewed as someone of no value, so they would put her out in the cold to die and then throw her body into the Ganges River. Such was the system that considered one group of people filthy simply because of the family of their birth. They were all trapped in a cage built 3,000 years ago, with no way out. I, even in my much more comfortable position, felt I was also trapped, bound by gender and tradition, and I determined to find my way out.

When I was about seven years of age, I told my mother I wanted to be a doctor. She took me to her brother's clinic so I could get a look at what doctors actually do. Her brother was a renowned radiologist and always had 50 to 100 patients waiting to see him. I was impressed by the fact that my uncle was able to help ailing and hurting people. I also loved the blessings that the patients gave him after their cure. But most of all, I was impressed by his white coat. How I longed to be able to wear a white coat like it some time in my life!

As we left, I informed my mother again, "I want to be a doctor."

She replied, "I will make that decision, not you." Those words told me I would have to fight to achieve my goal.

By the time I was ten, I knew the only way to free myself was through education, so I pursued my studies zealously. I wanted the freedom of Western girls, and I had to convince my mother to support my ambition. The only way I knew I to do this was through outstanding grades.

Prior to our move to Kanpur, I attended St. Mary's Convent in Allahabad. When we moved back to Kanpur, I attended a public school and instantly could tell the difference. I wanted to return to convent education, since all of the lessons were taught in English, and the nuns provided a much better education than the public schools did. What I didn't expect was my mother's opposition.

CHAPTER 4: The Trap of Tradition

"If you send me to the convent," I told her, "I will have better chances, growing up with English as a first language. That will open up more choices for me." I already knew that medical education was taught with English books, so anyone wanting to be a doctor had to know English.

"It is out of question," she told me. "What need do girls have of education? Your security is in finding a husband, you know."

"How will I find a husband? You tell me I'm not pretty like Manju."

"You are disrespectful as well. Do you not know we don't have the money for this school? It would take almost half of your father's income to send you there. Selfish, that's what you are."

My mother's comments weren't entirely fair. It was true that the tuition would eat up about 400 rupees of my father's salary of 1,400 rupees a month. But his job didn't merely provide him with a salary. In addition to his wages, his job paid for our housing, the telephone, transportation, and much of our household help. A convent education would take far less than half of his earnings.

It also grated on me how she harped on me at home about the difficulty of saving money for my dowry. "Don't think you'll stay here forever. You need to improve yourself so you can have a good arranged marriage. And how do you think we'll be able to find you a good husband without having a dowry for you? If we send you to that convent, we'll never be able to get you married off."

My mother's attitude was by no means unusual for that time, even though she knew from experience the value of education. Her father had arranged for her to be homeschooled until a school for girls opened. She was one of the first to be sent to school in a time when few girls of any caste were educated. Her father made sure she stayed in school long enough to be certified as a Montessori teacher, an achievement of which she was justifiably proud.

For my parents, educating girls was a way to cultivate higher minds and souls. They didn't want their daughters to grow up ignorant. However, they were frightened about our future, scared of their girls going into the world alone. They were right to be fearful. Life in India was frightening. People were prone to rob you on the street. Life was survival of the fittest, and no one trusted anybody. My parents wanted us to have husbands who would protect us amid the dangers and pitfalls of Indian life. I wanted an education that would get me out of India.

We battled for months. I badgered and nagged my mother to allow me to attend the convent. My father was willing that I go there; my mother wouldn't listen to anything he had to say on the subject. She felt the public school was good enough for a girl. Even today, many of the public schools in India are known for teachers who don't show up, poor quality teaching, and little discipline. I knew that kind of education wouldn't get me far.

My siblings also chimed in; at least, my sisters did. Mridul, the younger, was in favor, thinking that if I got to go to the convent school, she might also be able to. My older sister was opposed to my going. She resented the idea that I would be given a chance she didn't have.

By the time Mridul was old enough for the convent school, money wasn't so tight, so she was also able to attend. Because of the education we received there, we learned to speak better English than Manju ever did. I always felt bad about this. Manju deserved to have the same education Mridul and I did. With her keen intelligence, she would have made the most of it. She was especially brilliant in mathematics, and the schoolteacher in her came out as she tutored me in math for years, helping me pass my exams all the way up through the eighth grade.

My brother, of course, had no opinion. He, as the son, was the king of the house, but he was too busy with his own friends to bother with what the girls were doing. And there was no question of not paying large sums for his education. He attended St. Xavier's, the English medium school for boys, and no one begrudged one rupee of the cost. How I longed to live in a country that educated its girls as well as the boys! My deepest desire was to live free like the girls I saw in the UNICEF movies—girls who took education for granted as a birthright.

Several times my father's brothers, who were generals and colonels in the Indian military, visited our family. Over a meal of *purree* (fried dough) and mixed vegetables, they used these opportunities to encourage

CHAPTER 4: The Trap of Tradition

my parents to send me to the convent. My uncles' years in the military, which was patterned after the British model, had westernized many of their attitudes, including those about educating women.

"Give her a chance, Krishna, since she is so keen."

"But the money," my mother replied.

"Learning to speak English well is important. I see it all the time. Those who know and speak fluent English are promoted faster."

"She wants to be a doctor," my mother said, rolling her eyes. "She has no interest in military service."

These high-ranking officers were not defeated by their sister-in-law's objections. "That's fine, let her want that. English will help her succeed in medical school."

"And she's young," another put in. "She could change her mind. Knowing English would make her a candidate for the Indian Foreign Services or the Administrative Services. Jobs are starting to open up for women there. Anju could have a great future."

"I don't see why you are so insistent," my mother argued. "None of my sisters are sending their girls to convent schools, you know."

"That's up to them. But we are talking about your Anju."

On and on they sparred over my education. Finally, one of them managed to persuade my mother to agree. "Let her try," he said. "If she studies well and excels, then allow her to continue. If not, pull her out. But she deserves a chance, if she wants it so badly."

Even though I won this battle, it only served to solidify in my mother's mind the impression that I was the most disobedient and headstrong of her children. She was determined to make the best of it, though. Outside the home, to friends and relatives, she prattled about wanting to give her girls a good education so they wouldn't have to be dependent on men. She was proud of the fact that she could send her daughter to a convent school while none of her sisters could afford to do the same for their girls. Chin up, looking down her nose, she'd inform her sisters, "I do not have to worry about collecting dowry. I invested the money in education."

It was unusual at that time for girls to receive such an expensive education. Most middle-class families could not afford the tuition.

Many rich families thought they had the money to buy a good husband for their daughters by paying a large dowry, so they didn't see the need to pay for educating girls. Knowing she was doing something considered progressive, my mother babbled endlessly to the relatives about how wonderful it was that I was attending the convent. But in her heart, I knew she had doubts about the value of that education.

I was determined to prove her wrong. I was confident that, with hard work and prayer, I would make good use of the convent education. It would serve as a stepping-stone to my medical education, and from there, to freedom.

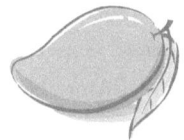

Chapter 5
My Key to Freedom

Proudly I put on my uniform: a white blouse, a tie, a navy-blue pleated skirt, black shoes, and white socks. After months of fighting with my mother, at last, at the age of eleven, I was starting at St Mary's Convent in Kanpur, operated by missionaries from Ireland and Germany, nuns who invested their lives in the girls who attended the school. Head held high, I walked about an eighth of a mile to the place where the navy-blue bus would come for me and the other girls from the neighborhood. Because we lived so far from the school, they had to pick us up at seven in the morning.

A nun always rode the bus to chaperone us, and she would lead us in saying the Hail Mary as we traveled an hour and a half. Arriving at the convent, we all had to kneel in front of the statue of Mary and do the sign of the cross. After prayers and assembly, we would go to our classes. The school day ended at 3:30, so it would be nearly five by the time I returned home. My father would come home, we'd play our games for a little while, and then I'd hit the books.

One of the fascinations of the convent school was the white skin of the nuns. It gave them an aura that created a sense of awe and wonder in me. In the summer they wore white habits; in the winter, black. Always they bore a rosary tied around their waists and a large wooden cross around their necks.

There was a certain hierarchy with the prefixes in the convent. Starting from Reverend Mother Superior, they descended through Reverend Mother, Mother, and Sister. Nuns of the first three groups always wrote "I.M.B.V." after their names, signifying an educational degree they had received from the Institute of the Blessed Virgin Mary in Ireland. There they had learned to live a sacrificial life in service outside their homeland, far from their families, to their dying day.

I was privileged to take a peek into their living quarters one day when nobody was around. I saw two nuns lived in a room, sleeping on bunk beds. They all used a common bathroom and kitchen. They ate simple foods, mostly the ones they grew in their vegetable garden. I also came to know that they would rise up at four in the morning to pray in the chapel until seven, when they received Holy Communion. They also prayed in the evening from seven to ten. They were holy and pious and gave me a reflection of piety, love, and grace.

More than the appearance of the nuns, it thrilled me to realize that I was living more like the children I had seen in the movies, the children my age in England and America. The school was clean with well-trimmed flowerbeds. Unlike the public schools, we had a lunchroom, a music room, a library, an infirmary, a sports field, and a basketball court. No unruly noise penetrated the grounds, and the girls always walked in a single line from the shortest to the tallest.

The convent teachers were strict and firm. While some of them were nuns, most were Indian women who spoke fluent English and were well versed in the subjects they taught. We were slapped on the hand if we used any language but English. They taught us composition, letter writing, English literature, history, mathematics, physics, chemistry, and a lot of what they called moral science, which for me was always the first lesson of the day. While the Catholic girls went to catechism, the rest of us—Hindus, Muslims, and Sikhs—to moral science.

In this class, we learned about the story of Creation, the plan of God for mankind, the Sermon on the Mount, and the parables of Jesus. In all of these lessons, the Gospel was never clearly presented. Some of the girls laughed at the moral science lessons. Others were a little offended by them. We all knew the convent education was the best we would be able to get and learning all this stuff about Christian thought was the price we had to pay. I simply memorized what they taught us. Little did I know how God would use these early seeds to plant faith in my heart.

One story that did catch my attention was the one in which a blind man came to Jesus asking to be healed. Jesus talked with the man, made a paste of dirt and spit, and rubbed it on the man's eyes. When the man washed it off as Jesus told him to do, he was healed. From early childhood I had heard that Jesus was a miracle worker. We knew that Jesus was a real man who actually lived, not some demigod with four hands or six feet, horns, or an elephant's trunk. I thought this story must be about a true miracle, not some myth or fairy tale.

The nuns taught us to learn by cramming, memorizing everything and saying it over and over. Since there were always so many people coming and going at my house, I never had a good place to study. I would walk around the garden, through the sweet-smelling beds of roses, past the ripening tomatoes and eggplant, now in the sun, now with the shadow of a banyan tree on my book, repeating aloud what I was trying to learn. One time I saw two vipers, reared up with their heads nearly two feet off the ground, entwined around each other, mating. With sweating hands and a pounding heart, I scurried away from them. That sight scared me, but not enough to stop me from studying—even in the garden.

Afternoons, our garden was often a busy place. As my father progressed in his job, he was able to work from home at times. His subordinates would come with him and sit in the garden, sipping tea, the staccato of the clicking keys of their typewriters merging with the chirping of the birds to provide background music to my murmured repetition.

The convent gave me other opportunities as well. The nuns encouraged us to put on plays, and over the years, we performed *Hamlet*, *The Merchant of Venice*, *Macbeth*, and many others by Shakespeare. I learned my lines the way I learned everything else—holding the book as I walked in the garden, one eye on the watch for snakes. Along with theater, I was in the debate club. It should be no surprise to anyone who knows me that I excelled in debate.

The nuns also urged us to compete in athletics. Even though I was short, I was a fast runner, and I ran a leg in the 1.5-mile baton relay. Through those competitions, I developed my love of exercise.

They also taught us painting, which I studied enthusiastically. I had always loved to create with colors: in drawings, embroidery, and cross-stitching. Painting was one interest my mother did support. She believed that prospective husbands would be impressed by an artistic girl.

Along with academics, athletics, and arts, the nuns taught leadership, morals, and hard work. The school divided all of the girls into four houses: red, blue, green, and yellow. These houses competed against each other in academics and sports. By the end of my senior year, I was the captain of the yellow house. Every morning we recited the school motto: "Nothing is achieved without labor." Each house had its own motto. The motto of the yellow house was "Truth alone triumphs." Repeating this motto daily impressed on me the need to speak the truth. What I didn't understand was the need to speak the truth *in love,* something that caused me great conflict without my understanding why.

Much of my time in those years was spent developing myself, whether through study, athletics, or art. I wasn't a very social person because I had the idea that jabbering like birds or gossiping or speaking ill of others weren't good things to do. I particularly remember that the nuns called girls who whispered and talked all the time and were inattentive to instructions "crackatinas." I determined never to be labeled as a crackatina, as I wanted to be held in high esteem by my peers and the nuns.

Several of the girls, like me, preferred to use their time in better ways. Those of us who were diligent, excelling in academics, sports, and arts, received "Good Girl" badges, became class monitors, and belonged to the League of Goodness. I still remember a time when I won four badges: First in Class, Good Girl, Class Monitor, and League of Goodness. I especially liked the League of Goodness badge, as it had an image of a burning candle on it, and the motto "So let your light shine." This award

CHAPTER 5: My Key to Freedom

made me very proud, and it fired my competitive spirit to earn those badges every month.

As I became more absorbed in my studies and activities, I spent less time with my siblings, paying little attention to them. In fact, years later Sudhir and Mridul told me that most of their memories of me were either of me crying to get my way or studying, keeping myself separate from the family. As a result, today I am not as bonded with them as they are with each other. Now I wish it could have been otherwise.

I attended the convent school from fourth through tenth grade, always with the same group of twenty-one girls. We grew up together, put on plays, and competed athletically. What we didn't share were our notes or study techniques. It was not common to help other students learn. Learning was a competition, as places in colleges and universities were limited. If you helped someone else, you could jeopardize your own future. I did, however, love telling the other girls about my brilliant marks.

I was very proud of myself and my accomplishments in school, soaking that education up like a sponge. When I finished eighth grade, I had to make some choices about my education. I knew the decision would impact my entry into medical school and potentially my whole life. At twelve years old, making this decision was both confusing and overwhelming.

Starting with the ninth grade, there were two tracks students could follow. The first was the Board of Education track, which concentrated on math and physics. The other was the Senior Cambridge Track, which followed a syllabus laid out by Cambridge University in England. This track was very prestigious and included much more in the way of English literature. Adding to my confusion, the Board of Education track covered only ninth and tenth grades, while the Cambridge track lasted three years, through the eleventh grade. I could do either of these options at the convent school.

Looking ahead, I knew that to get into medical school I needed to complete twelfth grade. Those who took the Cambridge track could do so by taking on one more year of school through an interscience school. Those who took the Board of Education track would have to take two years of interscience.

Because of my accomplishments, I was invited to participate in the Cambridge track. I wanted badly to take it. My mother, however, pointed out that if I finished the tenth grade through the Board of Education track, I would be eligible for a scholarship to the interscience school of about sixteen rupees a month, which would cover my tuition, leaving only my transportation and food for my parents to pay.

I shocked my mother by acceding to her wishes, probably for one of the few times in my life. While I would have liked to follow the Cambridge track, either one would help me achieve my ultimate goal of becoming a doctor. I knew without the scholarship, I was in for two years of daily battles with my mother over the tuition. I preferred to save those battles for the day I got into medical school—if, of course, that ever happened.

Chapter 6
One More Step to Freedom

The years in the convent school sped by. During this time, Sudhir started engineering school and left home to board there. This gave my mother a sense of security: her son was getting an education and was on his way to establishing a stable life. It also freed her up to focus on her three girls. In her mind, security for us was to get married.

During my last year at the convent school, I won first prize in the national science contest. I discovered a diuretic agent in some leaves by using a process of filtration and decantation. There was some medicinal value to this discovery, as it could be developed into a medicine that would help people with water retention problems. The prize awarded me a full scholarship to a university—if, and only if, I studied pure science.

My mother was pleased with this opportunity, as she thought a university education would improve my credentials for attracting a husband. It didn't matter to her what I studied. I kept insisting that I wanted to be a doctor. I didn't want the scholarship.

My announcement only led to more arguments. "Why should I pay for a medical education, Anju, if you can study for free? You are so self-centered." She had the ability to make even hot days feel cold just by the way she spoke to me.

"But I want to be a doctor."

"Medicine is not for women. That's what my brother, the doctor, always tells me. Why don't you listen to him?"

"There are women doctors."

"Oh, I am just a mother, not a Mother Superior. What do I know?" She glared at me, eyes narrowed and lips compressed. "You don't do what your parents want you to do. Why can't you study chemistry? You can get a university education that way. That should be good enough for you."

I knew my only chance to become a doctor was to study very, very hard. And study I did. When the electricity in the house went out, I would go outside and sit under a streetlight. Within minutes I would be covered in mosquitoes. I knew that I had to prove to my parents that if they invested in me, their money would not go to waste. Fear and anxiety chased all the what-ifs that whirled in my mind as if driven by a typhoon.

My mother's persistent nagging was like the whine of a mosquito—a whine that irritates not only by its sound but because you know sooner or later it will bite. Since direct appeals didn't change my mind, she switched to other tactics. "Stop that studying and help me in the kitchen. You are a girl; you need to learn how to do this. Otherwise, nobody will marry you."

Occasionally my father answered her. "No, she's a doctor, so she won't need to do household work." From his words, I knew my father had faith that I could succeed. My mother had no such confidence.

I finished the tenth grade as class valedictorian. To get into medical school, I had to complete the last two years of what was called ten plus two: ten years of schooling, plus two more of interscience.

Since I had gone as far as I could in the convent, I had to move on to interscience at a state school. This was almost like going to a foreign country. No more riding the bus for me, chaperoned by a nun. I took a rickshaw to school, pulled for at least an hour and a half through the streets of Kanpur. The rickshaw was a large tricycle with the driver up front, pedaling. The passengers sat on a plank between the back two wheels. I always pulled up the canopy to give some protection from the

CHAPTER 6: One More Step to Freedom

sun or rain and closed the curtain to shield me from the gaze of passersby so they wouldn't know a young girl was riding alone.

The rickshaw took me through the streets of the city; past the holy river; past shops piled one on another, crammed together; through the crush of buses, cars, rickshaws, carts pulled by oxen, people on foot, and the incessant sound of horns. The breeze brought hints of the tangy smell of the leather works, decaying refuse on the street, and the spices of cooking, insufficient to mask the diesel fumes and the stench of the rickshaw driver's dirty, stale sweat. I held a book on my knees, reciting my lessons to myself, trying not to think about how slowly the traffic was moving, wondering if I'd be late, feeling my irritation rise if the rickshaw driver wasn't pedaling fast.

At school, the contrast was even greater. In the convent, just as the walls surrounding the property kept out dangerous intruders, the nuns had protected and sheltered us from outside influences. They nurtured us and encouraged us to improve ourselves and our intellects. The girls with whom I had studied were among the brightest, and the teachers were dedicated and believed in challenging us.

Going to interscience was like being thrown into chaos. Some of the classes were taught in Hindi, which I wasn't used to. Next to no discipline existed, and the teachers came and went, with no more interest in us than the flies on the wall. Cheating was rampant. Girls would skip class to smoke, and they were open about having sex. I was scared of them.

"You behave like the English. Why aren't you Christian? Why do you call yourselves Hindu?" were some of the taunts they would throw at me and the other girls from the convent school. Saying we behaved like the English was accusing us of imitating those who had made the Indians slaves. The truth is, they were jealous: we had better style in dressing, won the favor of our teachers by our respectful behavior rather than flippancy, and in general had better manners and didn't use foul language. They also didn't like how we could speak in English to each other, and they couldn't understand us.

What bothered them most, I think, was that they knew we had parents who were interested in our lives and were willing to invest in our educations. Teasing and taunting, treating us as outcasts were their ways of expressing this jealousy. We convent girls stuck together, eating lunch together, forming our own clique.

More and more, I was looking ahead to the entrance exam for medical school. I didn't feel interscience was giving me adequate preparation for it, and I insisted that my mother hire private tutors for physics and chemistry.

"You don't need that," she said. "You only think of yourself. It's too expensive."

I cried and cried, begged and pleaded. Finally she gave in to my persistence, and yes, my nagging, simply to have some peace. Her capitulation came with an ultimatum. "You have one chance to get in. If you don't succeed the first time, that's it. You'll get no more help from me."

Once I had the tutors I needed, I had to struggle to find time and quiet enough to study so that I would pass my final exams with flying colors and be ready for the medical school entrance exam.

My mother put stones in my path every chance she got. The medical school exam was scheduled for June 30 and July 1. My mother organized Manju's wedding for July 2. "I don't care what exam you have," she told me. "The wedding is important, you know."

For weeks the whole house was full of relatives drinking tea and talking aimlessly, like the residents of a fool's paradise. The main topic of their chatter was my sister's intended. They discussed his family, the fact that they lived in Calcutta and owned a business, and the fact that he'd been to Germany.

"Did you know he ate beef when he was there?" one aunt said.

"What did he think of the taste?" another asked.

"I asked him. He said it was very tough."

"Maybe since he's been abroad, he'll take Manju. Such a good opportunity for her, to go to a foreign country."

"Did you know he wears Revlon cologne? Such a nice aroma."

"Has anyone gone to their house to see if it as big as they say?"

This was a valid question. One of the pitfalls of arranged marriages was that if the parties were from different cities, no one really knew if the families were telling the truth about their financial circumstances.

CHAPTER 6: One More Step to Freedom

"Oh, yes, my neighbor has a relative in Calcutta. She went to their home, met the family, and saw the house."

For hours they talked—about the wedding, the food, and the gifts. Then my mother and aunts began working, making the traditional pickled limes, papayas, and mangoes. They scurried about, making arrangements for someone to do laundry and clean the house and finding extra servants for the day of the wedding.

The bride's family pays for the wedding, even transportation for the groom's family and feeds them while they are there. I have vivid memories of Manju's in-laws demanding the luxuries they were used to, as well as their complaints that the mangoes were not ripe.

All of this is on top of the dowry the bride's family pays the groom's family. In return, the groom's family brings jewelry for the bride, which the bride's relatives inspect to make sure it is real gold. Manju received a lot of gold jewelry from her in-laws, so everyone was confident (unwisely, as it turned out) that she was marrying into a financially secure family.

I was desperate to escape all this banal chitchat and the endless small details and find a quiet place to study. No one dared ask me to get involved. They knew my answer would be some impolitely expressed variation of "Take a hike."

The rains had started some weeks before, so studying in the garden was impossible. Looking in all the rooms, at last I found my spot: the box room, where we stacked cartons of possessions we rarely used. I climbed up the pile and sat with my head nearly touching the ceiling, a bare light bulb illuminating my book. Sometimes rats or mice got trapped in that room and died, leaving the room reeking of their decaying corpses. When the stench became unbearable, I would get the household help to assist in my hunt for the dead one to get rid of it.

On both days of the exam, I got up early and wandered around the garden until I saw a blue jay. I hoped this powerful omen of good luck would help me pass. When I dragged home at the end of the second day, no one was interested in how I had done. I felt like a wilted flower no one wanted.

The next day was my sister's wedding. My mother set up a big white tent in the yard for the ceremony, and she decorated it elaborately with marigolds and gardenias, but the fierce rains caused it to collapse. All of the guests had to crowd into the house. The bridegroom arrived riding a white stallion, but the effect was somewhat spoiled because he had to carry an umbrella to shield himself from the monsoon.

I wasn't surprised that my mother was preoccupied with Manju's wedding. By getting married, Manju proved herself to be an obedient daughter, stepping into the role our culture expected her to.

I, on the other hand, was feverishly pursuing other goals. I wanted to flee the oppression of our culture like a prisoner longs to escape his jail cell, but I had to wait to find out if I had been successful in taking my next step toward freedom. The results of the entrance exam were due in the middle of August. The class in the local medical school would consist of eighty-two boys and eighteen girls. The year I took the exam a plethora of girls wanted to get in, so the competition was stiff. Plagued by anxiety over the outcome, my mother's nagging didn't help. "What are you going to do," she'd ask, "when you don't get into medical school? Have you thought about that?"

When my father's younger brother invited me to stay with his family, I jumped at the chance. What I didn't know was this uncle had an ulterior motive. I was nearly eighteen, good-looking, and spoke fluent English. My uncle and his wife wanted me to marry one of the officers in his regiment. Every evening, they urged me to dress up and go to the officers' mess with my uncle, giving the young bachelors a chance to flirt with me. To this day, that aunt holds a grudge because I didn't marry the man she picked out for me.

Finally mid-August arrived. I couldn't bear to wait to read the exam results in the newspaper. Instead, the evening before they were to be published, I went to the dean of the medical school's home, knowing he would have been notified earlier. I knocked on his front door, the hairs on my arm standing up, showing my terror that I had failed. Nervously I told him why I had come. He told me that not only had I passed, but I had scored sixth in the entire state. I fainted right there in his elegant

CHAPTER 6: One More Step to Freedom

parlor, collapsing on his ornate French provincial sofa. Such was my relief that I had not failed—that I still had a chance to escape.

Predictably, my mother was very happy that I got in. She took great pleasure in telling all the relatives about my success, as if she were responsible for it. "My Anju is in medical school," she would constantly remind anyone who would listen. "She's going to be a doctor, the first one among all her cousins." To me, her constant direction was, "Now you need to find a partner, a boy to study with, so you can marry him." I didn't think at seventeen I should feel so driven to marry.

Since I had scored so high on the exam, I had the opportunity to choose which medical school I would attend. I wanted to go to the one in Lucknow, about thirty-five kilometers away, which had a very good reputation, much better than the one in Kanpur. My mother put her foot down at that. She refused to give me the money to pay for boarding in Lucknow.

"We're paying your tuition, and that's enough. You can live at home," was her answer to any of my arguments. "We've spent all the money for your dowry on your education. We have nothing else for you." She shook a finger in my face. "You'll just have to hope someone falls in love with you. Then you can get married, and we won't have to pay a dowry."

Her words were bricks thrown through the bars of the cage that still held me, bricks that bruised my soul. My only way out was through excelling in medical school. I wasn't sure I could; I just knew I had to.

Chapter 7
The Study of Medicine

I tried to keep my expression bland as a few upperclassmen approached me from across the campus, walking through the avenues of oak and mango trees, past beds of dahlias, chrysanthemums, and poppies. During the first two weeks of medical school, the older students hazed the first years. We were expected to wear all-white clothes and walk with our heads down from one lecture theater to another, to the dissection rooms and labs, or to a hostel. Upperclassmen would approach us and say sarcastically, "Lift up your head; oh, aren't you beautiful." Then they laughed, mocking us. The boys faced even worse hazing.

Soon after I started medical school, I took advantage of my commute to think about my situation. I rode a rickshaw out of the city, along back roads through fields and rice paddies, traveling nearly an hour and a half each way. While I could use the time to study, the tedious journey was wearing and stressful. I was never late for class, but there was always the chance the rickshaw would break down or the driver would take his time.

The commute wasn't my only problem. At home I had to contend with a volatile atmosphere, fomented by my mother's nagging and criticism. How was I to study in these conditions?

CHAPTER 7: The Study of Medicine

One day I announced my solution to my mother. "I am going to move into the girls' hostel at the school."

"No, you aren't. You are too young to leave home."

"I am almost eighteen. Besides, there's too much disturbance at home. I can't study here."

"How can you say that? It's just your father and me, and Mridul. Besides, I'm not giving you the money."

"I can't get anything done here and am unprepared for my lessons. That's wasting the money you paid for my tuition." I literally banged my head against the wall and cried loudly. When my mother left, I locked myself in my room for several hours without food or water. I look back and wonder at myself for such behavior. But such was my desperation to get out of India and the lengths I would go to flee its constraints.

Not believing the work in medical school was that rigorous, my mother took me to see her brother, the doctor, thinking he could give me some useful tips for studying *Grey's Anatomy* or *The Cunningham Dissection Manual*. Then I would stop nagging her, to let me board away from home.

We sat in his opulently decorated parlor, complete with a marble fountain and a mural of deer grazing in a pasture that covered an entire wall. At one end of the parlor was a sunken section of marble, forming a separate sitting area.

My uncle took a seat on his white leather sofa. "There's nothing to the study of medicine," he told me, my mother nodding approvingly at my side.

"What?" I stared at him with wide eyes. All the signs of his wealth and success were intimidating to me, but what he was saying was completely contrary to my experience in medical school.

"I'll explain. If the patient has a throat infection, you call it tonsillitis. If he has a bowel infection, he has gastroenteritis. If it's a skin infection, dermatitis. And if the infection is in the eye, it's iritis. All you need to know is the *itis*."

So much for the uncle whose white coat had inspired me to become a doctor!

For months I battled my mother, using every possible means to get my way and her permission to move to the hostel. I would cry and scream, banging my head against the wall until I drew blood. Sometimes I refused to eat for four or five days, even if this meant watching my family enjoy a feast. Papa always had a soft spot in his heart for me, and he would beg me to eat something.

After a year of this stalemate, my father was unexpectedly transferred to Lucknow. As I could no longer live with my parents and attend medical school in Kanpur, they agreed that I should move into the hostel. There I shared a room with another girl and a bathroom with twelve others.

If I had a weekend off, I would sometimes come home, but often I'd stay at the hostel and study. It was so very hot, over 100° and very humid in the summers. All of the rooms were about eight by ten feet. We'd block the entrance to the room with a block of wood or stone and pour water on the tile floor to cover it a few inches deep, then run a fan on it to create artificial air conditioning. When even this brought no relief from the sticky, weighted air, I would go up to the rooftop and study well into the night.

By this time, my brother had married. His wife, Indira, like a good traditional Indian woman, was completely committed to the family into which she had married. Even though she toiled from morning to evening—cleaning her house, preparing meals, waiting on my brother—she also started taking care of me. Indira washed my clothes and sent food to me at lunchtime, knowing the food in the cafeteria was not only fattening but inedible. In her, I felt God had provided a guardian angel. Her love, care, kindness, and gentleness touched me deeply, as I had never before experienced them.

I also observed how Indira became the target of my mother's abuse. Mum-mee would stand on the veranda and rant about Indira to anyone around. "I was cheated by that woman, you know. She's too dark skinned, uneducated, and she didn't bring enough money as her dowry. A cheat, that's what her father is." My mother, who'd been so hurt by her own mother-in-law, treated her daughter-in-law still worse. This mistreatment scared me, as it made me certain that an abusive mother-

CHAPTER 7: The Study of Medicine

in-law was in my future if I married an Indian man who lived in India, in the vicinity of his parents.

During these years, I prayed to Santoshi Mata, the goddess who satisfies all your desires. I fasted every Friday for her, giving up citrus, salt, eggs, or any non-vegetarian food. I also prayed to Shankar, a male god whom I begged to provide me with a good husband. His day was Thursday. I would go to the temple to offer flowers, fruit, incense, and sweets and pray. I thought Santoshi Mata would get me to America, and Shankar would get me married to the right husband.

The five-and-a-half years I spent in medical school were a grueling race, the toughest season of my life. The program I attended compressed the usual first two years of lectures and labs into eighteen months. I had to give up sleep, consume lots of caffeine, and abandon any social activities to keep up with the pace. I did it all. I refused to give up on my goals.

Medical school stressed me in other ways. After years in girls-only schools, this was my first exposure to boys other than my brother and cousins. My parents never discussed anything related to sex, and I'd done my best to tune out the girls in interscience, so what I was learning about reproduction and virginity was eye-opening for me. It was difficult to know how to act when these topics were discussed, so I remained reserved and aloof.

Some of my classmates didn't like that I held apart, and they were offended that I didn't attend their parties and events. I became known as a walking *Grey's Anatomy*, and some of my classmates thought it would be funny to take me down a peg. Playing pranks on people was common in India. While the victims of the pranks were supposed to take them as jokes, there was often an underlying element of malice.

Many of the other students used amphetamines and illicit drugs to stay awake. Since they knew I never used these drugs, they thought it would be funny to give me a chance to try some. During my first year, they used the festival of Diwali as their opportunity.

Diwali is the Festival of Lights, signifying the light of knowledge that vanquishes ignorance. People hang mango leaves and marigolds over their doorways. The dark nights are lit up with fireworks and campfires in the streets. Many people exchange jewelry and sweets. So I thought nothing of it when some of my classmates came to my home and brought me some barfi, a sweet made of ground cashews and sugar. They made small talk, then left the second I took a bite of their offering.

Immediately I noticed a feeling of euphoria and psychedelic effects such as seeing multiple stars of multiple colors. I had a transcendental experience that was actually quite goofy. I felt I was lifted out of my body and saw little shining spots floating around. My body felt light; I wanted to giggle and laugh. I knew I had taken marijuana in the barfi and that my classmates had got me.

Things quickly got strange and unpleasant. I became fearful as I started seeing a rat with a ten-pound weight hanging from his tail. Every time I would put the weight on his tail, it would fall off. I thought this was a law of physics: that the tail of the rat was not stiff enough to hold ten pounds. I was sure I had lost my brain forever and that I would never graduate from medical school. Feeling useless, helpless, angry, and betrayed, I did not want to share my experiences with my family. Rather than wallow in anger at my classmates, I decided to go to sleep.

Twenty hours later, I woke up the next afternoon, feeling completely normal, hungry, and slightly lethargic. I never confronted my classmates because they would have denied knowing anything about an extra ingredient in the barfi. That bizarre transcendental experience was my first and last encounter with an ingestion of marijuana.

In month nineteen of medical school, the routine changed. Six days a week we would sit in class from eight to noon, then have a quick break for lunch followed by labs until four. From six to nine in the evening we were on the hospital wards, doing clinics with patients. I would go home to study until one or two in the morning, then try to get some sleep before I had to get up at six and start a new day. On Sundays we were free from classes or labs, but we still had to go to the wards.

The wards contained about forty metal-frame beds, all crammed together. If the patients wanted sheets or pillows, their families would have to bring them, and if they wanted to eat, the relatives had to provide food as well. Patients were coughing, wailing with pain, begging for the nurse to bring the bedpan. Because of so few nurses, the wards reeked of urine and feces, and bandages were rarely changed.

For clinics, we were divided into groups of four or five and assigned to demonstrators—medical graduates who were serving as residents in one of the major branches of medicine, such as internal medicine, pediatrics, or surgery. Each day the demonstrator would give us the next day's topic, saying something like, "Tomorrow we will study cirrhosis of the liver." That evening we would read up all about cirrhosis and liver function and everything else we thought we'd need to know. The next day we would all crowd around a patient, and one of us would be asked to take the patient's history. Then we would discuss the case. The demonstrator would fire questions at us. "The liver is enlarged. That could be cirrhosis; it could be something else. What other causes of liver enlargement could there be? How would you determine which it is?"

The dermatology clinic was held on a veranda outside of the hospital. We girls sat in a semicircle around the demonstrator; the boys stood behind on benches. We crowded together to form a curtain, screening the patients from the view of people's passing by.

The patients, many of whom had sexually transmitted diseases, sat on a wooden bench near the entrance to the veranda and waited for their names to be called. When summoned, the patient would stand in front of the demonstrator and us, the audience. The demonstrator would ask, "What is your major complaint?"

"I have a lesion," the patient would respond and point to his underwear.

"Take off your clothes." When the patient would hesitate, the demonstrator would continue. "Don't worry, they are all doctors." So the patient would have to disrobe, right there on the veranda, screened from the eyes of anyone around by the bodies of the medical students.

Along with being famous for leather, Kanpur also had the highest rate of tuberculosis in the world. Most of the patients we saw had the disease in one part of the body or another. The doctors assumed everyone they saw had it, unless proven otherwise. One patient I can never forget. I felt sympathy for his plight and helplessness that I could do nothing for him. He was sitting in the sunlight of the open-air hallway, waiting to see someone for his leprosy, surrounded by the other waiting patients, many of them coughing. Blood, feces, and urine soiled the floor. Listlessly, the man with leprosy stared straight ahead, as if oblivious to the people passing by and the maggots that were crawling out of his nose.

Scenes like this showed me the need to desensitize myself. I didn't have a problem with blood, urine, or stools. But when I saw patients vomiting—heard their retching, smelled the acrid odor—I would vomit as well. I had to tell myself that this reflex was not compassion; rather, it was weakness. I had to become stronger. Over and over I told myself, "*You cannot throw up,*" willing my stomach to obey me. Over time, I grew accustomed to the sights and smells of the clinics, the odors of human blood and waste mixed with harsh antiseptics.

In addition to TB, we saw a plethora of patients with leprosy, tetanus, hydrophobia, cholera, and hepatitis. Infectious disease was so prevalent that there was even a separate hospital for its treatment. Some of the most heartbreaking cases were infants. As part of a ceremonial rite, the umbilical cord would be cut using a thistle dipped in cow dung. Many of those babies would then contract tetanus. By the time their parents brought them to the hospital, they would be so dehydrated they had no chance to survive.

As part of our training, we observed surgeries. We carefully scrubbed our skin, dried our hands with hot air and sterile towels, and donned sterile gowns, caps, and masks. One day as I leaned over a patient undergoing a laparotomy, one of my long braids fell out of my cap and dangled over the patient's open belly. The surgeon cut off six inches of my braid with his surgical scissors and threw it onto the floor. He glared at me with flaring nostrils and wide eyes, shouting, "I am doing this to teach this girl a lesson for life." He was right; I never forgot that incident.

On top of the appalling condition of the patients, which was the fruit of poverty and ignorance, I saw the corruption of many of the doctors. Working in the state hospitals, they collected a salary from the government. The law permitted them to treat patients at home in their spare time for extra money. So if a well-dressed patient came to

CHAPTER 7: The Study of Medicine

the hospital, the doctor would instruct that person to come to his home in the evening to be treated there. Once the patient arrived, the doctor would squeeze cash out of him.

Many doctors had what were called *trouts*, young men who would stand at the train station looking for families bringing patients to town for treatment. They were easy to spot: the ill person would be crying out in pain, and lots of family would be hovering around. The trouts would take these people to the doctor. Then they would start trying to get all the money they could out of these people's pain and suffering.

Many people didn't understand that the doctors were simply trying to extort money from them. Others did, but they also knew the quality of care they would receive at the doctor's house would be far superior to what they would get in the hospital, where they would be just one of many patients competing for each doctor's attention.

There were other ways to get more money from the patients. For example, one common surgery was to remove tuberculomas, which are lymph nodes infected with tuberculosis. If the surgeon opened the patient and saw more than one tuberculoma, he would take off his gloves and walk out to the waiting room. "The price I quoted you," he'd tell the family, "was for one mass. Your relative has three. So my fee is three times what I told you. When you bring the rest of the money, I'll remove the masses."

The doctors' corruption didn't stop with how they treated the patients. Postgraduate students would work under these doctors twenty-four hours a day, seven days a week, getting their groceries or taking their children to school. If they refused to do these personal errands, they wouldn't be eligible for board certification.

All of this corruption left me feeling nauseated. I didn't want to practice medicine in such a money-hungry environment with no shred of ethics. I couldn't understand how the same culture that revered the sacrifices of Gandhi or the service of Mother Teresa would blatantly take advantage of others' distress. I wanted to live in a country that cared about all of its people, and I was sure I would find that in a land like America.

Most revolting to me were the obstetrics and gynecology wards. There were about twenty birthing stations with no curtains between them. The women labored there, lying on the delivery tables with their feet in the stirrups, hollering in pain as there was no anesthesia. Interns and second-year residents scurried around, trying to catch the babies as they were born, brushing away the flies that swarmed everywhere. Once one woman delivered, there was no chance to clean up the bed before another woman needed it.

All the placentas were collected in a bucket. Dogs would slink into the delivery room and eat the placentas, disturbing the flies that flew from the bucket to the instruments to the patients.

Compounding my horror at the conditions in obstetrics was the fact that at that time, women medical school graduates had a tendency to go into obstetrics. All of the obstetricians I knew were single because they could never make the time to get married and have children. They were expected to deliver fourteen to twenty babies a day, some of them by C-section. The more I saw, the more determined I was to get out of India.

Somehow I got through those years, even making time to play badminton for the university team and to perform in an amateur theater company. I graduated in 1975 with high praise from my teachers. The sketches I drew from *Grey's Anatomy* were put in the medical school's museum.

In all of this time, I hadn't fulfilled my mother's dream. It wasn't for lack of opportunity. Some of the demonstrators wanted me to marry one of their colleagues because they thought I had great potential. Many male students tried to talk to me, to strike up a friendship, to come to my home. They couldn't approach me directly for a date, so this was their way of hinting at what they wanted.

I did not want to consider any of those possibilities. I was thinking about my next step for getting to America. My goal was to break the shackles of the bondage I felt in India, to flee the social stigma of being a woman, and the battles I had to fight just to have a career. The only way to achieve this goal was to get out of India. America was my best chance.

CHAPTER 7: The Study of Medicine

Did I know a lot about America at that time? I thought I did because of those UNICEF films I had seen as a child. The films had told about the heritage of the United States, the presidents, the World Wars, but most of all about the produce. I dreamed about the fresh oranges and apples that grew in Florida. We learned to fill in the map of America with the names of the Great Lakes, the states, and their capitals. As I grew older, I started exploring what kind of an income a career in medicine would bring in overseas. I was sure if I could get to America, all my problems would be solved.

Some people I knew went to England, using that nation as a stepping-stone for getting to the United States. But there many encountered discrimination, as India had been a colony of the British, and Indian doctors were not readily accepted as colleagues. I didn't want to waste time in a country that might not give me opportunities. The quickest way to realize my dream was to take—and pass—the Educational Council for Foreign Medical Graduates exam. Then I would be able to apply for internships or residencies in the United States.

The problem for me was that the exam wasn't given anywhere in India. The closest place was Kuala Lumpur in Malaysia. I was jealous of the rich boys with whom I studied, whose parents gladly gave them the money to travel to take the exam. I knew my mother would never give me any money for such a purpose. Neither she nor my father understood that if they made that small investment in me, I could be more successful in America than I ever could in India.

So I knew I had to find yet another way.

Seth family (from left): Anjuli, age 8, Bhagwan, Sudhir, age 16, Krishna, Manju, age 12, (front) Mridul, age 4.

Our 25th wedding anniversary (from left): Zach, Nick, Luke, Anjuli, David.

Veranda of childhood home.

(top photo) St. Mary's Convent School.

(left photo) Motto on chalkboard at convent that stuck in my heart.

(top photo, next page) Luke's wedding (from left): Nick, Anjuli, Luke, Rachel, Marcia, Zach.

(bottom photo, next page) David's medical school graduation.

Our family, the year before my cancer (standing, from left): Dave, Zach, Luke, Nick, (seated): Alicia, Anjuli (top)

Anjuli and Dr. Wendy Stock. Photo by Jean Lachat. Photo courtesy of University of Chicago Medicine (right)

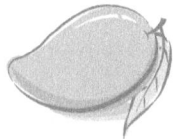

Chapter 8
Desires Granted; Hopes Destroyed

After I finished the coursework portion of medical school, I joined my parents in Lucknow and completed my year of internship at the better school there. All medical students had to intern for a year before graduating, rotating between medicine, surgery, gynecology, and social intervention medicine.

If I hadn't already decided I needed to get out of India, my experiences in social intervention medicine would have convinced me. We traveled on a bus to small villages and put up tents marked with a red triangle. Most women in the villages were illiterate, but everyone knew what that triangle meant: the gynecologists had arrived.

The conditions these village women endured defied belief. Most lived in mud houses that melted under the pounding monsoons. The only toilets were the fields where rice and vegetables were grown. The villagers had little to eat. They suffered from intestinal worms and often had raw wounds oozing with maggots. As the people had never been vaccinated, they were plagued with whooping cough, diphtheria, and tetanus, along with leprosy. Nearly all of them had tuberculosis of the lung or bone.

While the women came to us for relief from pain or infections with which they had suffered for months, we had another agenda. "How many children do you have?" was the standard question. "How many living? Do you want any more children?"

We would have the same conversation with them over and over. "No, I have enough," nearly every woman said. "I have one (or more) sons. But what can I do? Pregnancy is from God. If I don't get pregnant again, that will mean I don't have the blessing of the Almighty."

We would then get into a discussion of the menstrual cycle and when during the cycle pregnancy could occur. For most of them, this was a complete revelation.

But their answer was always the same. "I don't want any more children. But unless I have more sons, I am of no value to my husband. And I must be available for his pleasure. I cannot refuse him, no matter when in the month he wants to have me."

More women trapped in India's culture.

Unbeknownst to them, our agenda went deeper than simply educating them. In medical school, we were indoctrinated that no matter whom the patient was, our job was to control reproduction. The population was growing by leaps and bounds, and the government was concerned that the already overcrowded country with its widespread poverty would only get worse if the population growth was not limited. The goal was to alleviate poverty through providing food, clothing, shelter, and education for the citizens, but a rapidly increasing population made this goal seem almost unattainable. If poverty could not be alleviated, the thought was the people would rise up and ask why they were not better off now that they had been freed from slavery to the British. The resulting social unrest could convulse the country in violence and chaos.

If the women were educated, we could reason with them and encourage them to use their education to limit the size of their families. But we couldn't control the level of education in the villages, so we had strict instructions from our superiors on just what to do. If a woman had two or more living children, and at least one was a boy, we would sterilize her without telling her. All she would be told was that we had done surgery to correct whatever her presenting problem was. If we told her she could no longer have children, her husband would most likely beat

CHAPTER 8: Desires Granted; Hopes Destroyed

her and abandon her. If she was already pregnant and had two children, we were to terminate the pregnancy and tie her tubes. Some of these women didn't know they were expecting, and we didn't tell them. If a woman knew she was pregnant, we would convince her it wasn't a good idea to have the child. We coerced many such women to have abortions and have their tubes ties, all under local anesthesia.

It was dangerous to do such procedures in a tent in a field, cutting into the body and risking infection. Local anesthesia wasn't sufficient, so we supplemented it with ether—even though the ether had side effects like dizziness and vomiting. We had no means of monitoring blood pressure and no life-support equipment, not even IVs. Such were the lengths the government was willing to go to control the population. Ninety percent of India's population lived in these villages, and the government thought nothing of treating them like animals.

Population control had become an obsession for the government. By the time I was an adult, it was unusual for people in the literate classes to have more than two children. One was becoming the norm. People often ostracized relatives or friends who had more than two children. Third pregnancies were expected to be terminated. The government even came up with a slogan they printed on posters and plastered all over on buildings and buses: "Us two, our two."

I had survived the rigors of medical school, but I found the arduous pace of internship even more fatiguing. Adding to the drains on my physical and emotional energy, all my mother would talk to me about were different proposals of marriage. During my years in medical school, she pressured me to find a husband there. She would corner me when I was studying. "Since you couldn't find a suitable man to marry in medical school, I'll find one, and you will have to agree."

I would answer her without looking up from my book. "I will look at your proposals, but the final decision is mine." She would back off and try again another day.

As I grew older, her determination to marry me off intensified. Even before I had finished medical school, my mother took me to visit two men and their families, completely against my wishes. The first candidate wasn't a doctor, so I refused immediately. The second was from my class in medical school. Shortly after my parents received his proposal, his parents asked me to come to their home in Lucknow so they could interview me. This young man got on the same bus I was on. He never acknowledged me or offered to help me with my luggage—as if I didn't exist and as if he didn't know why I was on that bus. I thought if he treated me like that now, how would he treat me the rest of my life? I didn't want a man like that, one neither cordial nor warm. I knew I had to succeed in my residency, but my mother would never see any worth in me unless I married.

Mum-mee was undeterred by my refusals. Every day she would come up with someone. "How about this boy?" she'd say. "He has a college degree."

"No." That was my answer. If he was in India, I didn't want him. My plan was to marry someone already in America.

"Your expectations are too high. Who do you think you are? Do you think you are that beautiful and desirable that the perfect man will want you?"

Her words hurt. I had gained some weight because I was constantly studying and eating and had a little hump on my back from hours spent sitting on my bed, hunched over my books. Compared to my older sister, I had a dark complexion, which was considered a liability in a culture that prized lighter-colored skin, and I had acne as well. I was also flat-chested and not as pretty as Manju, who received all of the attention for her long hair and pale skin. All of these comparisons only added to the pressure I felt, pulled between my ambition of getting to America, my desire to marry someone who shared my goals, and an aching yearning for peace at home.

My mother knew the reason behind my refusals, and she had an answer for it. "And why are you so obsessed with going to America? If you do, you know you'll end up as a prostitute."

I always had to smile at that argument. My mother's limited knowledge of America came from movies. She thought every woman in America wore a bikini. In her view of the world, any woman who wore such a skimpy bathing suit must be a prostitute. Therefore, all women in America were prostitutes. She didn't want her daughter going to such a morally corrupt land to end up disgraced.

After every refusal, Mum-mee appealed to my father. "She doesn't want to listen to anyone." She pestered and harassed me with such hostility that I didn't want to come home. She would not talk about anything but marriage proposals, how imperative it was for me to get married, and that she wanted to be done with any responsibility to me. I felt like I was sitting on a time bomb that was about to explode.

I did have to admit to myself that all Manju's beautifying wasn't as silly as I had once thought. In fact, it showed she understood the trap in which we were born better than I did. In India, girls are merely a commodity and are in competition with each other for the best husbands. I had set my sights high, namely, a man already in America. I knew I'd have to pass the scrutiny of his parents or whoever was arranging his marriage, so I had to borrow some of Manju's wise strategy.

To make myself more desirable, I spent every free moment during my internship developing talents that might attract boys: cooking, painting, embroidery. During that year I finished thirty-two paintings, most of which my parents hung on the walls of our house. I also embroidered napkins, towels, placemats, and cocktail napkins, and I tatted yards of lace. The whole point was to improve my chances of catching a man who would bring me to the United States. Developing these talents was my way to beef up my image, to make me a more desirable product in the marriage market.

One day my mother was especially pleased with her find. Wearing a broad smile, she asked me, "How about this boy? His father is a doctor and has an established practice with room for the son. These people have money; they can pay to start your practice."

This announcement was the worst yet. If everything was as good as my mother made it sound, this boy would never leave India. A man from a poor family would be more likely to want to seek a better life somewhere else. "No," I responded. "I want to marry someone who lives in America."

Even though my mother thought I was impossible to please with my demands of a husband in the United States, she would not be defeated in her quest to marry me off. She continued to badger me inexorably with proposals, becoming increasingly angry at my refusals. Even my father felt I was being unreasonable.

In frustration, my parents placed an ad in the matrimonial column of the *Times of India*, the most circulated newspaper in the country at that time. To their delight, a family from New Delhi responded. "Our son, Divaker, is a second-year internal medicine resident at Methodist Hospital in Brooklyn." They said he would be in India for two weeks, and he had that much time to find his bride.

This time I said yes. This was what I had been waiting for. I prayed and hoped that he would like me.

Gleefully, my mother and father wrote a letter to Divaker's family. They enclosed a picture they had hired a professional to take of me, one where I was carefully made up, wearing my best sari and jewelry. They also included my curriculum vitae, describing my credentials for being a wife: the year I was born, my schooling, my grades, and hobbies.

To everyone's relief, Divaker announced that he liked my picture and wanted to meet me. He came to Lucknow on a Friday. Divaker wasn't much taller than I was, fair-skinned and balding. When I saw his pleasant looks, I thanked Santoshi Mata and Shankar for rewarding me for my fasts and prayers. I felt like I had won the lottery, and Divaker was the prize. He had everything I wanted: he was a doctor who lived in America, he was good-looking, and he wanted to marry me.

After a little conversation with my parents, Divaker asked my father if he could take me for a ride. It was unthinkable that we would be alone in a car together if we were not married. My father, not wanting to deny Divaker this request, arranged for a car with a chauffeur.

Divaker and I sat in the back as we drove around town. I clenched my hands together, trying to keep them from trembling. How desperately I wanted him to like me, to marry me, and to take me away from India.

"Anjuli, have you ever dated anyone before?" he asked.

"No, I never have." *Why did he ask me that?* I waited for him to ask me another question, but it never came. We rode in silence for a few minutes, the only sound the honking horns of the other vehicles. *What*

CHAPTER 8: Desires Granted; Hopes Destroyed

could I do to get this soft-spoken man to want me? I ran my hands along my arms, trying to flatten the hairs that were standing erect. "Do you like New York?" I asked him.

"I like it fine."

"Do you have time for the theater?"

"Not much."

"What is the hospital like?"

"Clean. Modern."

There was a pause as we passed a few rickshaws, and I tried to think of something to say. "Have you eaten beef?"

"Yes."

"How does it taste?"

"It is very chewy."

I could never have dared to eat beef in India. From the fact that he had defied tradition, I reasoned that he had broken the shackles of Indian culture and had embraced Western culture and its thinking. He was exactly the kind of husband I wanted.

As we drove around, we passed a temple. I asked Divaker if we could go in for a moment. He agreed. As I inhaled the aroma of incense and fresh flowers, I said a prayer in front of the idol: *God, let him say yes to me.*

The next day we received word from his parents. Divaker wanted to marry me, but he only had two weeks in India before he had to return to the States. My mother wasn't about to let that stop her, and by hustle and bustle, she got my wedding organized for the following Saturday, October 10. She kept talking about how much money this was costing the family, how she was spending a fortune on my wedding—forty thousand rupees, about $670.

That week, my father had a talk with me. "What if, Anjuli, he takes you to America and divorces you? What are you going to do?"

"Papa, I will jump that hurdle when it comes. Right now, I want to go to America." In truth, I barely listened to him. I couldn't imagine that divorce was in my future under any circumstances. I was convinced that getting to America would guarantee me a great life.

On the day of the wedding, my whole extended family came. I dressed carefully in a red and gold sari bought specially for the occasion. My mother gave me gold necklaces and red and gold bangles to wear. My face was painted with red and white dots. I had gone to a beauty salon to have my long hair arranged in an updo, and for the first time I wore eye shadow, lipstick, and high heels. For hours we ate the rich wedding food my mother had catered, surrounded by incense and fresh flowers. All of the guests wore vibrant, almost magical colors. Knowing what was to come, most of the guests left before the ceremony started.

A Brahmin pundit came to our house to perform the ceremony. The ceremony has not changed: the bride, the groom, the parents, and the pundit sit under a canopy, and the pundit speaks for hours in Sanskrit, which of course no one understands. My wedding ceremony started at eleven in the evening and went on till about four in the morning. As happens with weddings, most people other than the bride, the groom, and the pundit fell asleep. From time to time, the pundit gave his singsong instructions in English or Hindi. "Now offer the flowers, now offer the rice."

At one point, the bride's parents give the bride to her husband. That sparks lots of crying and wailing. "Now she's gone; she's no longer part of the family." I've seen it happen in weddings that the principles have to excuse themselves to use the bathroom or get something to eat. Other times, the pundit is bluntly told it's time to finish.

At last it ended. I was filled with hopes for the future, elated that I had found a husband who could take me to America. I hoped we could be happy together.

We had a one-day honeymoon in Kashmir, then Divaker took me to New Delhi to visit the Immigration and Naturalization Services in the American embassy so he could sponsor me as an immigrant. Then he was gone.

While I waited for my papers, we communicated solely by mail. In person he was quiet, almost boring, and his cut-and-dried letters were not much different. They were all the same. He was busy working and anticipating my arrival in New York. He never expressed any emotion.

CHAPTER 8: Desires Granted; Hopes Destroyed

The first three months of my marriage passed this way, from letter to letter. Even so, my sense of excitement grew as the day of my departure approached. America!

My papers came through, and I left India on the second of January, 1977. My Indian passport was stamped, "Left India for good." I breathed a sigh of relief—years' worth of relief. I had achieved my goal and had escaped the trap in which I had grown up. Now at last, new life could begin.

The plane trip to New York was adventure enough: I had never flown before. When I left the airplane, I could hardly comprehend this new country in which I had landed. It all seemed so magical: escalators that moved you from one floor to the next, doors that opened automatically, floors of granite, posters and murals all around. Brightly lit, the airport was a marvel of cleanliness and gleaming mirrors. I thought to myself, *America is so beautiful. Where do the prostitutes my mother talks about live?*

Wearing a turquoise-blue sari decorated with red and pink flowers and a gold chain around my neck, I felt out of place. My brown skin, untrimmed finger and toenails, and oiled hair also made me stand out, as did the traditional marks of a married woman: the red dot on my forehead and the crimson powder in the part of my hair. My palms and elbows were decorated with henna, and I wore red plastic bangles from my wrists to my elbows—more signs of a married Indian woman, but they made me feel conspicuous and out of place.

When I got to the baggage claim area, I found a cart and piled my luggage on it. After I cleared customs, I eagerly approached the fascinating escalator. Unsure of how to navigate it, I raised the cart, holding it tight against my chest and stepped onto the down escalator. At the bottom, the cart got stuck in the escalator, pulling me flat on top of it. The motion of the escalator ripped off my gold chain and flung it fifteen feet away.

People ran to assist me. One lady told me gently, "You know, you aren't supposed to bring those carts onto the escalators." I was embarrassed by my ignorance, and I hurried to retrieve all of my property, including the gold chain.

Divaker and his sister were waiting to meet me. He hugged me, then ushered me through the maze and wonder of JFK Airport. All of my papers were in order; I got my green card right there at the airport. My dream of leaving India had at last come true.

My husband took me to his studio apartment in Brooklyn, which was right across the street from Methodist Hospital, where he was completing his residency. There was one large room with the Murphy bed on one side, a small dinette, and a kitchen. He left me there, telling me he had to go to work.

I stood in the middle of the 650-square-foot studio apartment, surrounded by my luggage and a crate that contained four of my huge paintings, the ones I treasured above all the others—paintings I imagined hanging in my dream home. Feeling like my head had been cut from my body, I froze in place as my heart sank. My chest tightened, and I felt numbness and tingling in my hands and feet. I struggled to contain my anxiety. All I could think to do was pull my idols of Santoshi Mata and Shankar out of my luggage and set them upon the dressing table so I could ask for their blessing.

I tried to explore the apartment, but I did not know how to turn on a light switch, start the stove, or pull down the Murphy bed where I was to sleep. I looked in the refrigerator and saw a big stack of beer cans, some cheese, and assorted jams and jellies. There was also some salami that I took for raw meat.

I made myself a supper of cheese and bread. As there wasn't much else, I thought this might be the time to try alcohol. I'd never taken so much as a sip of alcohol in any form. I wanted to be an American, so I picked up a can of beer and drank down what I considered a truly American drink as fast as I could. Needless to say, between my exhaustion and the beer, I fell fast asleep on the carpet and remember waking up every two hours to visit the restroom.

In the morning, Divaker came back and showed me how to work the bed, the appliances, and the television. He picked up his workout clothes and departed for the gym. I felt abandoned and confused, and I couldn't figure out how to explain Divaker's behavior.

CHAPTER 8: Desires Granted; Hopes Destroyed

Over the next few weeks, I rarely saw him. He spent most nights at the hospital. Most of my time was spent alone in the apartment. Divaker's sister helped me learn to master the shower and the phone, showing me how to take the bus and where to shop for food and other things I needed.

I felt like a leaf plucked from a mango tree, wilting because I was separated from everything I had known before. I had no idea how to conduct myself. In India we only had loose tea, and I spent much time ripping apart tea bags to get enough leaves to make a full pot. The produce was a constant source of wonder. I had only known peas and beans from the garden. Vegetables in a can that didn't need to be sliced or shelled were a novelty for me. I had never eaten potato chips that were not homemade or drunk milk that did not need to be boiled.

Soon after I arrived, one of Divaker's coworkers invited us to a housewarming party at their apartment in the same complex. I wanted to buy them a $5 salt-and-pepper shaker set on sale for $1.50 that I had seen in the Mays shop window. Somehow I got up my nerve to attempt the bus by myself.

The bus was packed with people. I found a seat in the back. We were rolling down Brooklyn Avenue when suddenly there was screaming and hollering from the front of the bus. Two or three men wearing ski masks and holding guns were pushing people at the bus stop away from the bus. They got on, cursing, and one held his gun to the driver's head, ordering him to lock the doors and not stop for any red lights. Another started collecting wallets, jewelry, and watches. People were breaking windows to try to get out. Feeling that death was staring me in the face, I was terrified.

Somebody picked me up and pushed me out of the window. My elbow got stuck, and I dangled a few feet above the street. As I tried to free myself, I could hear the men yelling at the driver to take them to Kennedy Airport. I was dragged down the street as the bus started to move. Somehow I got my arm free, and I fell into a snowbank. Hysterical, I walked home. That night I saw myself on the evening news. I don't recall my husband's having anything to say about the incident.

My anxiety increased as the days passed and added up to weeks. I was studying to take the exam for foreign medical graduates, but the stress of my failing relationship with Divaker and his peculiar behavior made it impossible for me to concentrate. My hopes for a happy life in America were shattering little by little, like a rock struck with a chisel. How could my gods have disappointed me? I was aghast and bewildered. I knew from the little Divaker said that he had a lot of female friends and was popular with the nursing staff. None of this information relieved my uneasiness. Constant headaches plagued me. I found myself crying more and more and watching television to pass the time.

When he did come by, Divaker was aloof. He came to sleep in the apartment maybe two nights a week or simply to pick up his workout clothes or inform me he was moonlighting somewhere. Finally, after a few weeks, he told me what was going on. "My parents trapped me into this marriage," he said. "I don't want you; I feel no connection with you. This marriage is not right for me." He looked straight in my eyes. "Perhaps I am gay."

"But what about me?" In my shocked anger, I heard my father's warning echoing in my head. *What if he takes you to America and divorces you? What are you going to do?*

I could barely pay attention to what Divaker was telling me. "I'm going to moonlight for a while to make some extra money. When I have it, I'll give you $700 for a ticket back to India."

With that, he left me, the four walls of that apartment closing in on me like a vise. A hurricane of emotion swept over me: rejection, anger, depression. I felt totally devastated and wanted to kill myself. Who would help me? No one. I had no one to lean on. I was helpless, caught in a snare that was forcing me back to the prison I had so recently fled.

Chapter 9
Back in the Trap, but Not for Long

When I composed myself, I called my parents. It took a while for them to understand that my marriage was already over. "Are you sure?" my father asked.

"He told me he doesn't want to stay in this marriage."

Through her sobs, my mother said, "Just come back. Come home to your family." So after only two months in America, I was on another plane, headed back east.

I didn't go directly back to India. I couldn't face the humiliation. Word had already come to me that my relatives were gossiping about me, saying I had a personality conflict with my husband, that it was all my fault. Unable to face the faultfinding and blame, I stopped in Abu Dubai, where Manju was living with her husband. I thought maybe I could stay there, find work, and still escape India.

It wasn't to be. Manju wasn't sympathetic, and her husband was worse. After a week, realizing I had no alternative, I returned to India.

My first evening in India was spent at a guesthouse near the airport in New Delhi, where my parents and I stayed the night. Our time together was more like a shouting match than a welcome. "What did you do to make him dislike you so much?" my mother yelled at me.

"It wasn't my fault!"

"You must have done something. Did you insult him?"

"He said his parents forced him to marry me."

"You are lying. Why did he really divorce you?"

"I'm not lying! That's what he told me."

"He's just saying that. You have shamed us. You are to blame!"

All through this conversation, my parents were drinking a bottle of whiskey. After they had drunk for some time, they put Indian music on the gramophone and started dancing. I retreated to the bedroom, sulking and crying.

When she took a break from her merriment, my mother came into the bedroom. She sat down on the bed next to me and wrapped her arms around me. "I am so thankful, Anju, that he didn't kill you." This attempt to comfort was neither consoling nor loving, as it added more pain to my already raw soul.

When I didn't stop crying, she told me, "Okay, your love for America is now finished. You need to settle down, go into obstetrics, open a clinic. Otherwise, there is no hope for you. You'll be destitute. Then what will you do? Live off your brother in his house? Beg on the streets?"

I pulled away from her and buried my face in my hands, my shame preventing me from looking her in the face. "I don't want that. I want to be married."

"You do not need to get married in your life. Besides, who would want you now? A girl who was so distasteful to her husband that he got rid of her after less than two months? Everyone will think you have some terrible problem."

Instead of staying with my parents, I was sent to live with Divaker's. My mother thought this arrangement would look better. It wouldn't be so obvious that the marriage was over. They were cordial, kind, and generous, treating me with respect. Living with them gave me a glimmer of hope that there could be a reconciliation. At one point, Divaker's parents told me they were disappointed in their son and were going to do whatever they could to convince him to reconcile with me. As time went on, I knew that wasn't going to

CHAPTER 9: Back in the Trap, but Not for Long

happen. I stayed with them a few months. When they realized the situation was hopeless, I returned to my parents.

As if the collapse of my marriage was not traumatic enough, during this time a family member raped me. Thoughts of my failed marriage and the rape, which my parents refused to believe had happened, filled me with an overwhelming sense of guilt, shame, and worthlessness, engulfing me in darkness. I had nobody to talk to, no one with whom to share my feelings.

Distraught, desperate, on the verge of suicide, not knowing where to turn, I looked for help from God, trying to reach him through idols. I became ritualistic, fasting and chanting more and more. I developed my rituals. I would bathe the idol, dress it, offer it fruit and flowers. I would ring a bell, showing that my offering was from the heart. At night I would lay the idol down to sleep. I had always been told if I worshiped the idols and did what was right, they would reward me. I yearned desperately for whatever blessing they could grant me.

Having never dreamed that my husband would divorce me, I had never anticipated how my parents would respond to such an event. What I can't imagine is how they could have been less supportive than they actually were. They would have been far less upset had I been involved in a horrible, crippling accident. That at least would have had no shame attached to it.

Feelings are not discussed in our culture. Image and status are all-important. My mother did all she could to preserve them. I would hear her telling relatives and friends and neighbors that I had come home to India to study. She never let on to anyone that my marriage was broken.

My father and my brother went along with all of these lies. I knew they were trying to protect me from any worse stories being told. That was India. Never show your pain, always put up a good front so you are not vulnerable to others, don't give anyone room to criticize. Even close relatives were shut out in this way. Still, the lies hurt me, as did the fact that I couldn't talk to anyone about the inner turmoil, disappointment, and pain I was feeling.

For the next six months, I recuperated from the shock and devastation of my disastrous marriage. Its collapse was as devastating to me as if I had been in an accident where I had broken all of my bones and lost my eyesight.

I spent my time praying, chanting, and reading. Somehow I came across Norman Vincent Peale's book *The Power of Positive Thinking*, and I used what he taught to start making plans for my life again. Peale pointed out to me that although I was devastated, I was so much better off than a blind man, who could not even get to an elevator, press the right buttons, and get home. He stated that 285 million visually impaired people lived in the world, and of them, 39 million were totally blind. He gave the examples of Helen Keller and Joni Erickson Tada, describing their impairments, one blind and deaf, the other a quadriplegic. I drew courage from their lives, as I was not blind, deaf, or paralyzed. I had a good education, was healthy, and only twenty-three years old. Somehow, if those women could build productive lives for themselves, I could too. And in the process, I knew I had to leave the merciless restrictions of India—this time for good.

While I was trying to figure out my next means of escape, I took a job working for an acquaintance of my parents, an ob-gyn. Many teenagers and young women came to us, troubled that after eight or ten months of marriage they had not become pregnant. Since they had been married that long with no signs of a child on the way, they were considered infertile. We treated them the best we could. The usual solution? We would go find the nearest man, ward boy, doorman, whoever, give him a cup, and tell him to masturbate until he produced some sperm. Then we would lay the woman on a table and insert the sperm using a test tube—all in an attempt to help her conceive so her husband wouldn't beat or abuse her, and her mother-in-law would have one less thing to criticize.

I became more and more desperate to escape. The traps of caste, culture, and gender were unbearable, grinding me relentlessly down into despair. I had to get out. There was one more thing I could try.

What I did was write to our neighbor's son's wife, Smiti. She and her husband had been living in New York but had come to India for some further education. Smiti was compassionate and agreed to help me return to the United States, inviting me to stay with her until I got established. Since I already had a green card, all I needed was a plane ticket.

The only hitch in my plan was that I had no money. I needed help from my parents to get it. I worked on them for months, begging

CHAPTER 9: Back in the Trap, but Not for Long

and crying, sulking, isolating myself from everyone. They knew I was depressed, and they finally gave in to my arguments that my best chance for remaking my life was in America.

My brother agreed to lend me the money for the ticket, and he went to New Delhi with me to get it. The agent demanded US dollars. Undaunted, Sudhir took our rupees to the black market to exchange for dollars.

Once my father consented to my return to New York, he wrote a letter to an acquaintance of his, a Mr. K. P. Keswan, the consulate general of India in New York. In his letter, my father asked him to take care of me until I could become independent. Mr. Keswan responded that he would, and we let him know when my flight would arrive. Finally, on August 1, I left India again.

Sitting on the plane, I let out a long sigh of relief. I had been given a second chance. I had bolstered my courage and self-confidence, telling myself that if I worked hard, it would pay off. I was determined that things would turn out differently this time. To that end, while I still wore a sari, I wore none of the marks of a married woman.

I decided that America was now my homeland, for better or for worse. Just like I had applied myself to learn anything, I would learn how to fit in. This time I would not end up a crumpled mango leaf; this time I would be a sprig that grafts onto the new tree and thrives.

K. P. Keswan was a short, dark man. He met me at the airport and took me to his apartment in Queens. I stayed there for two days until Smiti called, saying she was ready for me to stay with her and her husband for the next month. I had made plans to take a coaching course that would help me pass the Educational Council for Foreign Medical Graduates exam, and the class would start in September. Smiti helped me find a place where I could stay as a paying guest with a Jewish woman named Rose Paragano. Living with Rose, I felt safe, at ease, and loved. I started seeing a ray of hope for my future, and I put my failed marriage behind me.

The coaching class was held at St. Barnabas Medical Center in Livingston, New Jersey. The course cost about $300. My sister Manju generously lent me the money to pay for it. If I passed the exam, I would qualify for residencies in U.S. hospitals.

I quickly made friends among the other students, as we all shared the common bond of being foreigners. Eight of us banded together to carpool back and forth to St Barnabas, crammed into a Volkswagen Beetle. I also met an Indian girl who became my roommate at Mrs. Paragano's, which cut down on my expenses. My roommate was married and had financial support from her husband, so she paid for my groceries. This camaraderie and kindness fed my growing sense of optimism.

I took the exam in December. By the end of February, my divorce was final. Divaker gave me $5000, and I received the results that I had passed the exam. Now I was on my way—free from my husband, free to start my career, free from India.

Only it wasn't that easy. Most residencies were already filled. I wrote hundreds of letters of application, but I am sure they ended up in the garbage. Finally, another friend of my father's was able to help. This man's name was Naseem Saddiqui, a Muslim married to an Iraqi woman named Nina. She had a friend who was a doctor at Jersey City Medical Center. Through these connections, I landed a residency in pediatrics. Receiving the news, I thought I had reached the seventh heaven. I was elated to have achieved this milestone, the last big hurdle before completing my final training.

During the months before my residency started, I worked at Sloan Kettering Hospital as a lab tech, and I had the good fortune to work with some visionary scholars like Robert Good, who were doing pioneering research in immunology. They gave me the vision and planted the seeds in my heart to pursue immunology as a specialty. The idea of conducting research and being part of a major breakthrough in science and treatment seized my imagination. First, I had to complete my residency. After that, I was determined to follow my dreams.

I thought I was finally free of the oppression of my birth country. What I did not count on was the fact that while I was physically out of India, I was still Indian, and I still belonged to an Indian family. My mother continually harassed me to get remarried. At least twice a week I received long letters from her, usually between six and eight pages. In them, she complained that

CHAPTER 9: Back in the Trap, but Not for Long

she didn't want to shame herself by having to tell people I was divorced. If I remarried, she would act like I had always been married to the second husband and never mention the first. Anyone who noticed the different name would be informed they were mistaken. She pressured me; she tried to manipulate me to give in to her desires. She didn't give me any time to breathe, to get myself together emotionally after all I'd been through. She thought that since I was in America, I'd automatically become a millionaire. In reality, I was earning $425 every two weeks. Even though my room and board didn't cost much, I could barely save a nickel.

In addition, life as a resident was physically exhausting. We worked in thirty-six-hour shifts, six in the morning straight through to six the following evening, took twelve hours off, and went back to it again.

I tried to explain this to my parents. "I'm only twenty-three. Couldn't you wait three years until I finish my residency?"

My parents didn't want to listen. "You should have married at nineteen," they told me. "We can't wait until you are twenty-six. You'll be an old maid by then. No one will want you."

Then there was the money I'd borrowed from my siblings. "When will you pay back Sudhir? Manju? You owe them hundreds of dollars, and there you are making all kinds of money. Why haven't you paid them?" As is common in India, parents expect their children to support them. Usually they turn to their sons, but in this case they had me, the rich daughter in America. "And why don't you send us any money? Think of all we spent on you, on your education, your wedding. We can't take living in this poverty anymore."

Letter after letter, phone call after phone call, the nagging never stopped. My mother wrote long letters, pestering me about the $700 my brother had loaned me for my plane ticket, the $300 Manju had loaned me for the coaching course, and how I needed to return the money. Each letter was an anvil falling on my head, every phone call a stone hurled against my soul. I wanted to enjoy my residency, make peace with myself, form some friendships, and explore the city. I wanted a new life, but it seemed I was bound to the old one.

Faced with what they thought was my uncooperative and undutiful attitude, my parents even threatened to send my brother to advise me.

When I realized Sudhir was really going to come to America, I became desperate for some relief. So I put an advertisement in the matrimonial column of the *India Abroad* newspaper in New York.

In the second round of responses, I received a letter from a man named Ajit Nayak, saying he was interested in my credentials and wanted to meet me. I hoped this breakthrough had come in time.

Ajit lived in Galesburg, Illinois, working in emergency medicine. He called me, and we spoke for some time. Tired of Americans mispronouncing his name, he had legally changed it to Nicholas, or Nick for short, thinking that would be easy for both Americans and Indians to say.

In the course of our first conversation, he told me that his brother had recently committed suicide. Nick had been engaged to the younger sister of his sister-in-law, but after his brother's death, that relationship had fallen apart. His parents, who had come to America, insisted this disaster had happened because Nick's brother had married an American. They made sure Nick didn't marry his sister-in-law, demanded that he marry an Indian girl, and refused to leave the United States until that happened.

I appreciated how open Nick was about his past and that he was willing to overlook the stigma and stain attached to me for being a divorced woman. His gentle voice and open-minded attitude captivated me. We began to talk on the phone regularly.

Then he flew to New Jersey to meet me. Immediately I was struck by his good looks. Later, I was impressed at how concerned he was that I had enjoyed my dinner at the Raga Indian restaurant in New York City, where he took me on our first date. He came a few other weekends, always taking me to discos like Studio 54 or expensive places to eat. At the time I was living in Murdoch Hall, the nurses' dorm attached to St. Barnabas, where no men were allowed. The doorkeeper made an exception for me and allowed Nick to pick me up right at my room.

Between these dates, we talked on the phone nearly every day. I brought up my divorce several times, wanting to be sure I could believe that I was acceptable to him in spite of it.

"I do not care, Anjuli," he would say. "It doesn't matter to me if you're divorced."

CHAPTER 9: Back in the Trap, but Not for Long

I would stare at the phone in amazement. I couldn't make sense of this. American culture was more accepting of divorced people, but an Indian man? Even if the man himself had no objection, most families would never agree.

Another oddity about Nick was the gold cross he always wore around his neck, even though he professed to be a Hindu. I asked him why he wore it.

"A friend of mine gave it to me, and it protects me," was his answer.

When my brother arrived from India a few weeks later, Sudhir and I traveled to Fort Wayne, Indiana, to meet with Nick and his parents. Nick seemed infatuated with my communication skills, intellect, confidence, and looks. We were only in Fort Wayne for a day and a half, but during that time, Nick told my brother he wanted to marry me and have a really big wedding.

Nick's parents were reluctant to give their consent for him to marry a divorced woman, and one who was not from their ethnic group. My family was Hindi, from northern India. Nick's family, from Mumbai in the south, was Marathi, another of India's several hundred ethnic groups. They also had questions about the dowry. Sudhir promised Nick a big dowry. I was scared when Nick told me about this agreement because I knew the promise was hogwash. My parents had made it perfectly clear the money for my dowry was long gone, paid out in the form of tuition. I didn't say anything to Nick about it. I wasn't sure what would happen, but in the end, Nick's parents realized he was determined to marry me, so they gave their consent.

While I was thrilled Nick wanted to get married, I shied away from the idea of a big wedding. I didn't want crowds of people there, talking about my first marriage, or relatives demanding things of me. At last I prevailed, and he agreed to a small wedding. Nick was smart enough to understand that if we needed to have a small wedding, the dowry he had been promised probably didn't exist. If none of my relatives came from India for the wedding, how would the dowry be delivered? To my relief, this realization didn't seem to bother him.

His parents insisted that we marry in front of an idol of Ganesh, so we found a temple in New York that had one. My parents were not there, nor were any of my family, as my brother needed to return to India. A friend of mine gave me away, saying he'd be my brother for the day.

Again I wore a red and gold sari, red and white dots on my face, gold jewelry around my neck and along the part in my hair, earrings and a nose ring, bangles on my wrists. Nick wore white trousers and a peach shirt. Both of us had flowers draped around our neck. The pundit came wearing his white suit with a magenta turban. Since he had to take the subway to get home that evening, he timed the ceremony to finish in plenty of time so he could catch the last train at midnight. Thankfully, that schedule meant he spoke for only two or three hours.

Before leaving, the pundit changed into street clothes and removed his turban. He stopped by the receiving line to congratulate us. Nick, not recognizing him, asked, "Who are you?"

The pundit's face reddened. "I'm the one who's been talking to you the last few hours—the guy who married you."

The next day we took Nick's parents to the airport, as they were finally returning to India after seeing their son get married to a bona fide Indian woman. Then we took a flight to Niagara Falls for our honeymoon. There we stayed at a Best Western on the Canadian side. Nick kept talking about his cousin who lived in Toronto. "His wife looks just like you; you have to meet her." Nick was so insistent that, even though I thought it was ridiculous, I agreed to make the several-hour drive to his cousin's house. On the way I asked if we'd spend the night. I was feeling a little uncomfortable at the thought of spending the first night of my honeymoon at his cousin's place. Nick laughed at that question and assured me we would only stay a few hours. I was relieved, but that didn't lessen my sense of the absurdity of the whole trip.

When we arrived, they were busy watching a Toronto Maple Leafs game. The cousin's wife was heavyset with a charming face. She spoke fluent English and welcomed me to her home, but it was clear she and her husband would really rather be watching the hockey game. She informed me that she had cooked dinner, and it was on the table. After we ate and made some small talk, Nick and I left. Once in the car, I asked

CHAPTER 9: Back in the Trap, but Not for Long

Nick, "How do you think I look like his wife? She has a pretty face, but I don't think we resemble each other in any other way."

"Oh, it's not physical. It's more the way you both speak English."

I didn't realize it then, but a few years later, I figured out that the whole motivation for that trip was for Nick to show off his pretty wife who was a doctor and spoke fluent English. Nick and this cousin had a friendly rivalry about their achievements in life, and I was Nick's premium accomplishment.

The next day we decided to eat Chinese food for dinner. Around ten that night, while we were opening our fortune cookies, we heard a lot of screaming and yelling. Guys in ski masks and red gloves ran in and started shooting the bottles in the bar. The waitresses got on the floor and started praying. It should have been shades of the bus all over again, or even of my childhood encounter with the thief. Instead, I thought, *Oh, it's a Chinese floor show,* and I moved my chair so I could see better.

Three or four of the robbers cut the cords on the pay phones and closed the doors. Then one of them started collecting everyone's wallets, cursing as he moved up and down the room. Nick started shuffling credit cards out of his wallet, and within seconds, one of the robbers held a gun to Nick's head.

I couldn't breathe. I thought, *I'm going to be a widow on my honeymoon.* They took Nick's wallet, which had twenty-five credit cards, mostly for gas companies. Once they'd taken all of the wallets, they fled. Fortunately, I'd left my purse and jewelry under the bed at the hotel.

The next day, we all had to go to the police station. They declared they had never had a robbery like that in Niagara Falls, ever. Nick was adamant that we leave that day. He didn't have any of the numbers for the credit cards, and he wanted to go home to stop them. So my honeymoon ended on the third day. I didn't really get a chance to enjoy the falls.

I was beginning to wonder. With such a beginning, would this marriage have a chance to work out or not? Years later, Nick and I went back and had a romantic dinner by the falls, and I could laugh at my fears for the future, feeling confident in the life I had made for myself.

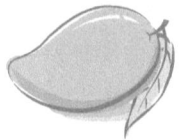

Chapter 10
A New Life Times Two

After the wedding, I moved to Illinois to join Nick. I was able to finish the last two years of my residency at the University of Illinois in Peoria while Nick worked in emergency rooms in Galesburg and Peoria, and we bought a house in Peoria in November of 1979. Our family grew quickly. David was born in May of 1980 and Zachary in 1984.

When David was six months old, my in-laws came for a visit. Nick's father would sit for hours, rocking the cradle, drinking Chivas Regal, cigarette in hand, blowing smoke in the baby's face. As a pediatrician, I was learning all about secondhand smoke, and I tried to get him to stop. He understood enough English to know what I was asking him to do, but my words meant as much to him as if a cockroach had uttered them. Daughters-in-law were peons in the family, not to be taken seriously.

Wives weren't much better. Most of what my father-in-law said to his wife, Indu, were food orders. At least, that was all I could understand of the Marathi language they spoke.

In this cultural difference lay the source of much of the conflict between us. I spoke Hindi, and they spoke Marathi—languages as different as Spanish and Swahili. Indu spoke no English at all. At the wedding, we all spoke in Hindi, but as time went on, Indu refused to

CHAPTER 10: A New Life Times Two

speak it with me. This was her way of ostracizing me, of keeping me in my place. My father-in-law knew enough English to insult me. He would start his sentence in Marathi to emphasize he was speaking to Indu and then say the last two words in English, so I would understand: "She's a worthless woman."

Some of the Marathi traditions seemed odd or even exotic to me. Traditionally, when a woman marries into a Marathi family, she takes on her husband's last name, as in many cultures. In addition, she takes her husband's first name as her middle name. Then her husband gives her a new first name. So not only do women get a new last name, but an entirely new name, reflecting their new identity. My father-in-law rarely used the name he had given his bride, Shamma, because she was used to being called Indu.

Nick's mother was a traditional Indian wife, and she expected everyone in the family to adhere to their assigned roles. She had been horrified when Nick had become engaged to an American girl. I was at least Indian. Nick's family was Brahmin, the highest caste, so my mother-in-law had already made a concession in accepting me. But visiting us was the real shock. As Nick says, "My mother found out I had married a coconut: brown on the outside, white on the inside."

Years of higher education and living in America had changed me. By moving to America, this branch from a mango tree had cut herself off, as though I had grafted myself onto a maple. Nurtured by Western thinking, I became more firm in rejecting the idea that I had to be second-class simply because I was born female, an idea I had never been able to accept anyway. For many Indians, mine was a radical concept imported from the West. Indu, without the benefit of education, simply could not see beyond the traditions to which she had been born.

Even though I worked all day, Indu insisted that I cook for her and wait on her. She complained to Nick that I was disrespectful and rude for not doing so, a very poor excuse for a daughter-in-law. For my part, I felt that since I was working all day, it wasn't unreasonable for me to feel she could prepare her own lunch.

77

Nick tried to help me out. "You cook very well," he would tell his mother. "Why don't you cook for us all?" My mother-in-law would have none of it.

To make peace, Nick took her on endless shopping trips, a task I couldn't do because I didn't understand a word Indu said. Much of what she bought was beauty supplies: shampoo, combs, rollers, permanent solution, dyes. Nick's sister Geeta, back in Mumbai, was setting up a beauty shop. Nick ended up purchasing a lot of her stock, items his mother carried back to India. We sometimes wondered what the real reason for their visit was. Was it more important for Nick's parents to see their grandson or to buy beauty items for Geeta's business? Later Nick's sister displayed them in her shop and made lots of money as her customers loved the Revlon brand.

While my mother-in-law was frustrated by a daughter-in-law she couldn't understand, I was repulsed by her bigotry. "How do you recognize all these white people?" she asked me through Nick. "They all look alike." Sometimes I would let comments like this go. At other times, I would talk back in English—certainly not what a good Marathi daughter-in-law should do.

At one point during their stay, Nick had a professional meeting in New Orleans, and we decided to take everyone. Indu refused to eat in any restaurants, as it was all American food, so we had to bring food for her to cook during our three-day drive. We packed a steam kettle and bought shrimp and yogurt, butter and spices. My sweet Nick peeled those shrimp in the hotel rooms in which we stayed along the way.

When we arrived in New Orleans, we checked into the plush Fairmont Hotel. Indu had stashed her food supplies in one of her bags, but she didn't think about the effect of the Louisiana heat on them. As the bellhop pushed the cart piled with our luggage to the elevator, I cringed as I watched the drip-drip-drip of melted butter making a trail of spots along the red carpet.

Nick's parents wanted to stay with us until May, but I was going insane, feeling like I needed to jump into a fire. After a busy day of

CHAPTER 10: A New Life Times Two

residency at the hospital, I wanted to come home and enjoy my husband and son, not wait on a nagging mother-in-law.

Then my in-laws came up with a new demand. They cornered me in the kitchen while I was serving them lentils and homemade chipatis. "We have decided," my father-in-law announced, "that we are going to take the baby to India and rear him there."

I froze, clenching the serving platter in my hands. "Absolutely not," I said.

"Why not? You are never home; you are a bad mother. Who is watching the baby, some hired girls?"

Carefully setting down the platter, I struggled to remain calm. "I'm completing my residency. Once I'm done, I'll have more free time and be home more."

"You need to choose between your residency and your baby."

For weeks the argument raged. Nick even went so far to get a passport for David. I was distraught. How could he even think of letting his parents take our baby? Nick had some friends who had sent their baby to be reared by grandparents, as the parents were both residents. This idea was unthinkable and incomprehensible to me.

Finally, Rosie, the wife of Nick's partner, came to my rescue. With tears in her eyes, she promised my in-laws she would set up a nursery in her home and care for David when I was at work. My in-laws accepted that plan, but they said they wouldn't leave until they were sure I had enough help.

Later Rosie told me they needed to leave my house immediately, and she helped Nick understand the stress I had been under. He took his parents out to look for an apartment. His mother told him, "Baba and I can't stay alone in one of these places."

"Then you'll have to go back to India," he told her. They finally left in March, just two months before David's first birthday.

A few months later, my in-laws insisted that we come to India, to Mumbai, to be married in front of their family idol. Most Brahmins had an idol unique to their family. Out of respect for them, we finally agreed to make the trip in 1982 when David was about eighteen months old. Then

79

the requests came in. "Could you bring this, could you bring that?" We felt like pack mules, loaded with still more shampoo, nail polish, and hair dyes. Imagine our dismay when we unpacked and found some of the bottles of shampoo had leaked all over the clothes we were bringing as gifts!

Nick's parents dressed us in traditional Marathi clothing. For me, that meant a nine-yard sari, instead of the usual six yards of silk. It also wrapped between the legs instead of simply forming a skirt. Then they led us to the family idol named Katyanibaneshwar. The idol was a little statue that was half-male, half-female. Again, my modern American life crept into my response to the event. I couldn't help thinking that I had learned in medical school that people who are half-male, half-female are called *hermaphrodites*. *Surely,* I thought, *they can't expect me to worship a hermaphrodite.* I went through with the ceremony, offering the fruit and flowers at the appropriate times, but not for the first time, I questioned what I was doing bowing down to little statues. When I later asked Nick about Katyanibaneshwar's gender, he said he had never even looked at the idol; he had merely gone through the motions.

Toward the end of our stay with my in-laws, Nick's sister washed my hair in her beauty salon. By the time we were on the plane, I knew that along with the three of us, we were bringing ten thousand undocumented immigrants in the form of head lice. Once we landed, we made a trip to the pharmacy before we even went home.

In spite of the lice, ours was a wonderful trip. For the first time in my life, I'd had a vacation with my husband and was able to see my family. Since we were financially secure, we could do a lot of shopping. Nick took me all over Bombay in a cab, showing me the affluent downtown areas and his medical school. We ate exotic brunches—that had over sixty items on the menu—at five-star hotels. We bought handmade jewelry, ivory tusks, and decorative items made of sandalwood. We walked along the seashore, the long curve of the bay lined with high-rises whose lights at night formed what was called Queen Victoria's necklace, our faces turned to the fresh breeze from the sea. India with Nick was very different from India without him—perhaps because I knew that I no longer lived there, and my life was no longer bound to this country's ways.

CHAPTER 10: A New Life Times Two

When I finished my residency, I joined a group private practice in Peoria and stayed with them for almost a year and a half before starting my own practice. I enjoyed pediatrics, but I still had my dream of becoming an immunologist.

In 1985, I was accepted into an allergy fellowship at the University of San Antonio in Texas. Nick was supportive of my going, even though he would have to stay behind, so I packed up my two boys and we moved south. By this time we'd been married almost seven years. At that time, Nick's priorities were work and money. He was physically exhausted from the hours he put in, so his temper was short, and he would yell and scream at the least provocation. He made all of the decisions about buying a house and the furniture. I was growing depressed because I felt I was still in that trap, oppressed by the culture I had tried so hard to escape—the culture that allowed men to suppress their wives.

In San Antonio I hired a babysitter to watch the boys while I was at work. Nick visited at least once a month, but I couldn't help feeling abandoned and alone. Still, I saw higher education as the way to keep myself out of the traps with which I had grown up, the snares of poverty and dependence. This inner conflict between striving for my goals and feeling forsaken tormented me, as if I were pulling a brand-new designer boot onto one foot while slowly sawing off the other.

On one of my rotations, I met Maria Falcon, who was a pediatric resident. I felt a connection with her. Even though she was Mexican, we had similar roots. Maria knew what growing up poor meant, and she understood the value of hard work.

We got to talking about life. I shared with her how Nick and I were arguing about David's schooling. He did not want David to attend a private school, even though we had the money for it. From that topic, Maria and I moved on to more personal issues. I could tell her about my abusive in-laws and the burdens of my life. "I have such a horrible life," I told her.

"Why do you feel sorry for yourself?" Maria told me. "You shouldn't. You are very attractive, you speak good English, you have a family. I don't know what your problem is. I also come from a non-English-speaking family that didn't have money. We spent the summers breaking our backs cutting grapes. You should look on the positive side."

She invited me to her parents' home in the Rio Grande Valley. I saw how her father mowed yards for a living, how the house in which she had grown up was similar to mine in India. I was amazed at how honest she was about her roots. *Where did she get this self-assurance—that she didn't worry that people would look down on her for her poor upbringing?*

To bolster my confidence, she helped me buy clothes or use makeup. One day she commented that she thought I would look better with shorter hair. That night I went to the mall and got a cute, short cut. Another time she suggested a second ear piercing. Same thing. I went to the mall and got one. Both times, when she saw what I had done, she said, "I was just making suggestions, not telling you what to do." I told her I wanted to do those things. But Maria knew that while these changes could help me, they didn't address my real issues.

From time to time, Maria would point out to me that my thinking was bizarre. I had developed an inferiority complex, feeling despondent about myself because of my failed marriage and the disapproval of my in-laws. Sometimes I felt as if I had brought it on myself, and I was starting to believe lies that I did not have any self-worth. I would say, "Poor me," or "I'm always unlucky. Why do horrible things happen to me?"

Maria listened intently to me, and she explained that some of my internal and external communications were not appropriate. "You need to think about these things, Anjuli," she'd tell me. "Feeling sorry for yourself or believing you are worthless won't help you live a happy life."

But I was good at pretending, and I hid behind boasting. For so many years I had only thought of myself, and that strategy had been successful for getting what I thought I wanted out of life. Maria knew of a better way. "Come to my Bible study," she urged me.

I didn't see how that would be of any use. My metal, wood, and stone idols sat in a small temple I had brought with me from India. I had set it up in a corner of my bedroom and decorated it with fresh flowers. Every morning and evening I carried out my rituals without fail. I burnt incense, chanted, sang worship songs, and constantly repeated lines of

CHAPTER 10: A New Life Times Two

the Holy Scriptures from the Gita and Ramayana as I prayed to my gods. I even sat my two small sons on the floor in front of the little temple as I worshiped.

Every time Maria invited me to her Bible study, I would have an excuse. I would schedule some moonlighting, working an extra shift. Or I would outright lie, telling her I was moonlighting when I wasn't.

Finally one day she gently said to me, "I know you can join us on Monday night. Why don't you come? We have good desserts."

"I'll come if you pick me up," I told her, thinking she wouldn't.

She agreed, and she arrived promptly at the agreed-upon time on Monday evening.

I am not sure what I was expecting, but an atmosphere of love, peace, and calm wasn't it. The people in the Bible study were all people to whom I could relate—doctors and dentists. They met in the home of a dentist and his wife. The home was simply furnished, not ostentatious, which helped put me at ease.

We gathered around the dining room table, and I settled into a seat, prepared to listen politely but sure they had nothing they could tell me. They were reading from the book of Acts. Everybody would read a verse and share what they had learned about God from it.

My heart was racing, and my hands were shaking as my turn approached. I hadn't been planning to participate! All I wanted to do was read the verse and get out of there. The verses I was to read were Acts 2:38 and 39: "Peter replied, 'Repent and be baptized every one of you, in the name of Jesus Christ for the forgiveness of your sins. And you will receive the gift of the Holy Spirit. The promise is for you and your children and for all that are far off—for all whom the Lord our God will call.'"

The pastor asked me, "What do you learn from that Scripture?"

I looked up from the book in my hands and said, "Not a thing. I do not know the meaning of 'repent' and 'baptized.'" I was puzzled by what I had read, and I sincerely wanted to know what it meant.

My response didn't seem to trouble them. They simply pointed to one Scripture after another to help me learn more, right from the Bible.

After they showed me several verses, I understood that repentance meant confession of your sins and a desire to turn from them.

One of them asked me if I had ever sinned. I hung my head, trembling. "As a matter of fact, I have sinned many times. The burden of my sins is enormous and is weighing me down." I was astonished that I was able to share with this group that I had sinned. I never could have been that open with anyone in India. I was hoping they wouldn't want to know my specific sins and publicly shame me.

The pastor spoke to me gently. "Jesus can forgive all of your sins."

This didn't seem possible to me. I was reared in a yin and yang system. If you sinned or wronged anyone, you appeased the idols by offering them food, money, incense, or flowers so that awful things would not happen to you as a result of your sin. "What do I have to do to be forgiven?"

"Nothing." I was shocked to know I did not have to do anything and that my sins would go away. I expected to be punished. This news was like raising a curtain from my eyes. I never imagined there could be such an easy solution! I wondered if somehow these people had an ulterior motive for telling me these things.

Maria, who was sitting next to me, saw my distress. She took my clammy hands in hers and stroked them gently. This was becoming more surreal every minute. Here I was, airing my dirty laundry, and all Maria could do was extend love to me.

So I asked the question again. Every person in the room stated that forgiveness was a free gift. Finally they convinced me.

"So what do I have do?"

"All you have to do is to invite Jesus into your heart, believing with faith that He has forgiven your sins, and there is no price you can pay for it. Jesus paid for it all by dying on the cross."

Then I asked, "What is the difference between Jesus and Gandhi and Mother Teresa? And what about the demigods and idols I worship? How are they different from Jesus?"

"None of them conquered death. Jesus rose from the grave because God resurrected Him. That's how you know He paid the price for your sins."

CHAPTER 10: A New Life Times Two

This explanation made sense to me, since I remembered hearing about an empty tomb from the nuns at the convent.

Then the pastor asked me, "What other idols do you worship?"

"I know that if I worship Satan, he will stay out of my life. I feed him and worship him and the evil forces so they will stay far away from me."

The group led me through Scriptures in the book of Isaiah, sharing how graven images are useless and have no power over life and death. They patiently took me through the Bible, showing me what God says about idols. That they spent so much time on my questions astounded me. They freely abandoned their agenda to minister to me. As they spoke, all the reverence and awe I had for my idols seemed to disappear. They were no longer holy and sacred to me, but instead became powerless pieces of wood and stone.

I was also struck by how open this group was when they shared prayer requests. No pretense, no hiding. One couple shared about their infertility problems, and a young man and his girlfriend talked about the struggles they were having maintaining sexual purity. Another man talked about how he had adopted two children from Vietnam and had raised money to bring over some of their relatives. The boat sank, and all were drowned. These people mourned with each other, encouraged each other, and prayed for each other with no condemnation or criticism. I had never experienced love and acceptance like this in my life.

Before I left, they gave me a Bible to keep and told me to read the book of John. My mind reeling, I started reading that Bible the minute I got home. I was overcome with a sense of peace and joy I had never experienced in my life, like a heavy yoke had been lifted from my shoulders. A sense of calm surrounded me like a wool shawl.

I thought about the love the people at the Bible study showed for each other. As a Hindu, I had been taught to keep my sorrows and burdens to myself. I could only confide in my idols, which indeed allowed me to share my feelings and difficulties, but they had little to say in return. I was so fearful of showing any shortcomings to anyone. I so longed for a community of people who would listen and encourage me.

85

The discussion of repentance flooded back as well. I had never seen myself as much of a sinner, and I thought my soul was pure. Now I realized I needed to ask for forgiveness. I read from John until the early hours of the morning. I didn't know exactly what was happening, but now I know it was the redemptive power of the Holy Spirit at work.

The first thing I did the next morning was summon up all the courage I had and collect all my idols, put them in a garbage bag, and get them out of my house. I can't believe I found the boldness to do such a drastic thing, as I suspected I might be struck dead! But the minute the idols were in the trash, I felt an inner peace and calmness, and I realized those little statues could no longer control me. I felt redeemed and aware that those evil forces were gone from my life. Joy took their place, refreshing my soul like a cool breeze on a stifling summer day.

I could hardly wait until the next time I saw Maria. I explained how I had thrown away my idols. "I want to become a Christian and be baptized," I told her.

Her eyes and smile widened. "Oh, yes, that's a very good idea. You should go talk to a pastor." Thankfully, I knew just who to talk to. I had been dropping my children off at the Sunday school at the Oak Hills Road Church of Christ whenever I had rounds on Sundays and didn't have a babysitter. Everyone there was so welcoming to me, inviting me to come to church. I had always give them a lame excuse like I had to work or some such reason. I decided to go talk to their pastor.

In the meantime, I called Nick. My heart was pounding as I dialed his number. I knew he would never approve of my becoming a Christian, as he was a Brahmin, the only son of a priestly family. What would he say? Would he be angry?

Once he answered the phone, I blurted out my news. "Nick, I want to be a Christian and get baptized." The Holy Spirit must have been talking to him, for his response was, "Go right ahead. In fact, since I'm coming there on Friday, I'll come to your baptism."

My knees went weak, and I dropped to the floor. Sitting on the carpet, I told Nick the entire story of my experience at the Bible study.

CHAPTER 10: A New Life Times Two

He said, "I know Maria, and she is a genuine lady. She would never lead you to a wrong place."

Surprised and pleased, I made an appointment to meet with the pastor. On Saturday, I met with him in his office at the church. He was a little surprised at my decision. "Are you completely sure you want to do this?"

"Yes, yes, I am sure." I looked across his desk into his eyes and nodded.

"But it's been less than a week since you heard what Christianity is all about."

"I've read a lot in the Bible, and I'm sure."

He looked at me, full of concern. Then he asked me all kinds of questions about my understanding of salvation and the meaning of baptism. Due to all of my Bible reading that week, I was able to answer every one. That Sunday in October of 1985 I was baptized, witnessed by Nick, Maria, my babysitter, and my sons. I felt the Holy Spirit enter my heart—a true rebirth.

I began attending Bible studies and reading the Bible more. Many Christian friends surrounded me and gave me Bible commentaries and books on how to read the Bible. Reading the Bible was like taking a drink of cool water after walking for hours on a hot and dusty road with nothing but salt water to drink. I started thinking about enrolling in some classes to learn more about the Bible, but that desire of my heart was not to be fulfilled at that time. When I finished my fellowship in June of 1987, Nick drove the boys and me back to Illinois, bringing along my new faith.

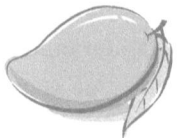

Chapter 11
Growing Pains

Back in Illinois I felt lost, uprooted from the nurturing of the church I had begun to call home. I was once again like a twig plucked from a mango tree. I needed to find a new tree to graft onto.

We moved to Bloomington, where I opened my allergy practice. I found a church I liked, but Nick wasn't interested in attending. Often we'd take the boys to Chicago for the weekend, and we'd attend Willow Creek Church. Nick started to buy the audiotapes on topics like how to manage money, how to improve your character, how to care for your family the church produced. He would listen to these tapes as he commuted to work in Peoria. I asked Nick if we could move closer to Chicago so we could attend Willow Creek more often, but he didn't want to leave his job.

Then I started attending a church in Bloomington, but Nick didn't like it. There had been some controversy there, and I was asked for my medical opinion about it. I was later quoted as saying the exact opposite of what I had said, which served to cover up a potential scandal. That I was used in this deception seemed like rank hypocrisy to Nick, and I had to agree with him.

Then a patient of mine invited me to Eastview Christian Church, and after visiting a few times, I started to attend regularly. A year or

CHAPTER 11: Growing Pains

so later we met a couple who had been missionaries in India, Bob and Sandy Knapp. They reached out to us and nurtured us.

All during this time I hosted weekly Bible studies in my home. I also joined Bible Study Fellowship. I simply could not get enough of the Word of God. I enrolled my boys in the Bible Study Fellowship children's program. They would do their homework faster than I would, and I so enjoyed that time of growing with them.

Nick, however, withdrew from all of this outreach. He wouldn't go to church, and when the Bible study met, he would go to the basement. When the study was over and the group was socializing, Nick would join us, his upbringing as an Indian taking over, forcing him to play his role as the host, the man of the house. He was always amazed that these people would come to our house for a Christian Bible study and be so warm to him, even though he was a Hindu.

I started to seek spiritual unity with my husband. I wanted him to have the light I had and to have the new perspective on life and eternity that I did. However, the words I used were not gentle and kind but harsh and abrasive. Seeing this, my Christian friends gently tutored me in the faith, teaching me how the fruit of the Spirit needed to manifest in my life.

That they were right was self-evident. Much of the drama of my life was disappearing in ways I could never make happen on my own. I used to lose my cool over little things, yelling and screaming at my office staff, my children, and my husband. I would even berate my staff in front of patients. I had seen surgeons do that but never thought about how the staff must feel. I realized that behavior was uncalled-for and that I would literally need to bite my tongue if that's what I needed to do to stop it.

Friends taught me about prayer, the need to turn things over to God. I was impulsive and made decisions ahead of God, without consulting Him. I had always prayed for help, for things like taking an exam—in India, getting help and protection was the whole reason we worshiped our gods. But as a Hindu, I wouldn't pray about certain matters, like starting a new project, forgiving someone, or simply feeling bad that I thought I could have done better with a patient. I struggled with considerable guilt and had to learn to give it over to God.

I had also stereotyped people—whites, blacks, Mexicans—because that's how it is done in India. I grew up believing that all Americans are happy; they live in the present moment and don't think of the future. The discrimination of the caste system was embedded in my blood, so I assumed that due to my dark skin, I would not be accepted or even touched by white people. I realized my stereotypes were wrong when white women whose husbands were farmers, women I would have expected to keep a dark foreigner at arm's length, freely embraced me with their love. Again and again my new friends told me that Jesus died for all—white, black, Mexican, Indian.

From my new friends, I learned how I should rear my children—without the criticism and scolding that I had received as a child—but with love, support, and discipline. The nucleus of my life started to change because of the love and care of these women. There was so much confusion in my mind due to my upbringing as a Hindu. I was reared to believe that my parents had the utmost authority on truth, and that by listening to them, I could learn this truth. The Hindu Scriptures were only used to appease idols, not to teach a way of life. My mother, for example, would tell me not to lie. Then I would hear her tell a lie, and I was confused by the double standard and uncertain nature of truth. It was hard for me to know what truth was. In contrast, the Bible should be used as our source and guide, not any person. I felt like I did when I was in medical school, soaking up everything I could learn. This time, what I was learning had eternal consequences.

My Christian friends also taught me how a wife should relate to her husband, and they were good at admonishing me about how I talked to Nick. They told me to read the letter of Peter which addresses wives' needing a gentle and quiet spirit, winning their unbelieving husbands not through words but through loving actions.

This teaching captured me, and I decided that instead of imposing my new faith on Nick, I would simply pray. Six-year-old David and I became very close during this time. We would go for walks on the Constitution Trail, and as we walked, we prayed for Nick to become a Christian. One day David told me that we are only strangers in this

CHAPTER 11: Growing Pains

world. I was so blessed that his faith was growing so deep. After we prayed, he would pick flowers and give them to me. I delighted in those dandelions as if they were roses or orchids.

As I wrestled through my many questions and the circumstances of life, the community around me told me never to lose faith, to keep praying. In the meantime, I had my struggles with self-centeredness and my need to control everything. I kept attacking these sins with Scriptures, praying for the Holy Spirit to transform me.

In 1991 my prayers were answered. Nick decided to convert. For many years, long before he ever met me, he had wanted to be like Jesus but had resisted the idea of renouncing Hinduism. Finally he did so and was baptized. He became engaged with rearing our children, getting involved with the church. I thought we would finally have peaceful lives.

How wrong I was! One victory in life often leads to new struggles. My ongoing battle with my in-laws intensified. They had always been critical of me. After I converted, they had a new reason to find fault. Nick's conversion turned that battle into an all-out war. My mother, who was visiting us at the time of Nick's baptism, was the first to give them the news. She called Indu and announced, "Your son has become a Christian."

"I don't believe it," my mother-in-law told her. "You are lying to me. Nick would never become a Christian."

"He did convert," my mother told her.

"This is just what your daughter says. I won't believe it until he is baptized."

"He did get baptized."

"How do you know?"

"I was there. I saw him get baptized."

My in-laws were furious. In Brahmin families, the role of the son is to worship his parents after they have died. Since Nick's only brother had died years earlier, that was to be Nick's duty. Obviously, as a Christian, he wouldn't perform the rituals his parents expected of him. Katyanibaneshwar would be without worshipers, to the great shame of the family.

After that, I did not allow my in-laws to come to visit for more than twenty years. On top of how abusive they were to me, I didn't want my sons around a man whose daily vices included smoking three-and-a-half packs of cigarettes and drinking a liter of hard liquor. I was afraid to have such a man around my children, and I didn't want them to see their alcoholic grandfather.

From time to time, my in-laws demanded that we bring the boys to India to perform the thread ceremony. "It doesn't matter that you say you are Christians," Indu would say. "You have to do this." We never agreed.

They didn't realize that given a choice, neither of my boys would have wanted to participate in a Hindu ceremony. Zach, my quiet middle child, was also growing in his faith. His teachers always said how polite and well-mannered he was, always following the Golden Rule. He participated eagerly in Bible Study Fellowship and AWANA. One year he won the Timothy Award for being the best student in the state of Illinois for Scripture memorization. For that achievement, he won a free trip to a Christian summer camp.

One Christmas, soon after he'd been baptized, he participated in the Living Christmas Tree at church. Zach was an angel, and Nick was one of the magi. They'd stand outside the church in their places, every night for five nights from five to eleven in the evening.

One night when he came home, Zach asked me, "Mom, are there any brown angels in heaven?" I was very moved as I realized that in this nearly all-white community in which we lived, the consciousness of racism had already touched my six-year-old son.

"Yes, Zach, there are brown angels in heaven," I told him. "God has made all angels equal, whether they are white, black, brown, or yellow."

Despite the conflict with his parents, Nick would continue to go to India every year to spend a week or two with them. He always came back with a heavy heart. His father was an alcoholic with uncontrolled diabetes and dementia. His mother was caring for him. Nick always felt he wasn't doing enough for his parents, which was what his mother told him. In reality, he bought his parents a condo, paid for household help

CHAPTER 11: Growing Pains

for his mother, and sent generous gifts of money. His father drank most of the money away. Nothing was ever good enough.

My mother-in-law approved of me for only two things. The first was that my complexion was lighter than Nick's, what she would call "fair." The second was that I had borne three boys, having given birth to Luke in 1993. Had I borne all girls, Indu would have felt justified in thinking me a completely worthless woman. But having three boys was something any Indian mother-in-law was forced to respect.

I was forty when I had Luke, and I felt I had been given a living doll with whom to play. We always treated him royally, giving him everything he wanted. He was so cute with his curly dark hair, and I enjoyed everything about him. Early on, I took him to church. He must have only been about eighteen months old when we asked him to sing us a song at the dinner table. Sitting in his high chair, he burst into "Little Children Belong to God." I was shocked that this little boy who couldn't speak in sentences was able to sing the entire song!

By this time, I had sponsored my parents and my siblings to come to the United States as permanent residents. None of them could comprehend my new faith or why I'd converted, or why I was rearing my sons as Christians. Tension ran high between us every time the subject came up.

Despite the tension, my siblings became curious about my newfound faith, and we'd have extended discussions over the phone. One Sunday morning, Manju asked me over the phone why I had become a Christian. I told her about the forgiveness of sin we can have in Christ. "Manju, we all have sinned and need forgiveness."

"Oh, I've never sinned."

The hair stood up on my arm and my jaw dropped, hearing what seemed to me to be a blatant lie. I gripped the phone a little tighter. "You mean you have never sinned in your life?"

"Oh, I have, but I am clean. I serve my mother-in-law, doing everything she requires. I will even wash her feet and drink the water I used if she wants me to. That's the service I give her. Because of that, my sins are gone." What could I say to that?

My family became even more displeased when they learned we were donating money to the church and other Christian causes. Some of them wrote letters to the church, saying Nick and I were unstable and that the leadership of the church had taken advantage of our instability, enticing us to convert simply because they wanted our money. They also said that I had always been a very spiritual person, and they were not surprised that I had joined a Christian cult. I had to work to forgive them for this interference and for the way they vented their wrath and anger over our giving our money to other people—not just them.

The family conflict came to a head in 1995, when I hosted a fiftieth wedding anniversary celebration for my parents at my house. Even though I had requested that they smoke outside, my brothers-in-law smoked heavily indoors. I couldn't get my sisters to try to convince them to go outside. I was boiling, angry at their disrespect, and I finally blew. This confrontation was the start of a feud that would last for sixteen years.

In spite of this, Nick and I pressed on, growing in our faith. We had to learn a whole different view of marriage than what we had grown up with. My parents had been married almost fifty years, and I watched them argue with one another every single day. This behavior made me believe that marriage is full of struggles and conflict. That constant state of conflict binds two people together with a lock and throws away the key. I never understood marriage as a loving commitment, in which I should consider the needs of my husband over my own.

Nick, for his part, had no concept of what it means to please one's wife. He had never had a father who led, as his own father was never involved with his family. His father thought only of himself, and when he was drunk, he would beat the children. His mousy mother simply chitter-chattered all day long.

We attended marriage seminars, and over time the Holy Spirit healed us of wounds from our pasts, both of us learning how to love each other the way Jesus intended for us to love each other. I would sometimes ask Nick what had changed. His answer was always the same: "Jesus has worked in me."

CHAPTER 11: Growing Pains

There were times Nick felt defeated and wouldn't want to attend church, but instead he would spend the time in contemplation of the Word of God. I realized that he was still able to teach the boys, giving them strategies for coping with life. He would get directly to the point and talk through issues, while he relied on me to keep praying.

We also struggled with leadership roles. In 1995 we went into practice together, with my doing most of the clinical work and Nick heading up the research. I was boss and doctor at work, and I had to come home and be wife and mother. Finally I learned that while I was the "general," as my boys called me, the one who issued orders and made things happen, Nick was the president—the one really in charge.

As the years went on, we settled into our routine of treating patients, managing the practice, rearing our three boys. I was in demand as a speaker and traveled internationally to speak at medical conferences. We began to support missions, getting involved with trips to Russia and India, supporting many good works among the poor.

In all of these endeavors, I continued to see the faithfulness of God in my soul, His joy and love. One major change occurred in 2001, as I was finally able to forgive the family member who had raped me. I wrote him a letter telling him so. This ability to forgive from my heart was only possible because of the forgiveness Jesus had extended to me. Before I had become a Christian, I didn't think it would be possible to forgive him; now I was flooded with peace and a sense of freedom.

As my boys grew older, Nick and I did all we could to set them on the right path. David and Zach finished college and entered medical school, David became engaged to a lovely girl, and our practice was busy, successful, and rewarding. We thought God had brought us to a peaceful place that would last forever.

Then the day came when I received the diagnosis of acute lymphoblastic leukemia. I knew nothing would ever be the same again.

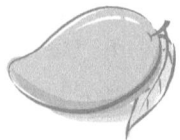

Chapter 12
Making Decisions in a Whirlwind

I had thought my life was a whirlwind, what with managing my medical practice, a full speaking schedule, travel, missions trips, my family, my home. All of those priorities faded to insignificance, paling before The Diagnosis. *Leukemia.* I could not think of anything else.

Why, God, why would You do this? As I sank into a bog of self-pity, the phone slipped from my hand and fell to the floor of my car. Jesus's words rang in my head: "Get behind me, Satan."

I sat up and shook my head. All of this self-pity was from Satan. I needed to cling to God. I swallowed hard and prayed for strength. Then I called Nick. In the few hours between tests, my white count had risen by eight thousand. There was no mistake. We had to accept the fact that we had a medical emergency on our hands.

That afternoon Nick and I went over to the cancer center and met with Dr. Joeng, the oncologist. He performed a bone marrow biopsy so we could get a more specific diagnosis. We knew we were dealing with some form of acute leukemia. Which one would determine the treatment—and my prognosis. In my heart, I knew already what I had. The tests would only confirm it.

By late afternoon, my three boys had arrived in Bloomington. Zach, then a third-year medical student, picked up Luke from high school

CHAPTER 12: Making Decisions in a Whirlwind

in Aurora on his way. David, a first-year internal medicine resident in Chicago, drove directly home, bringing his wife, Alicia.

Later David and Nick picked up the slides of my bone marrow from the oncologist and drove them to Champaign, about fifty miles away. There a hematopathologist, a physician who specializes in interpreting lab results of the blood, reviewed my blood samples. After the consultation, David called me and confirmed that with 80 percent blast (abnormal) cells, I had leukemia. I didn't need the hematopathologist's opinion to know that, but I had been hoping maybe there was some alternative. He also delivered some additional bad news. The specific form of leukemia was acute undifferentiated leukemia. Of the options, this was the one I didn't want. This form of the disease is highly aggressive, moving quickly into the brain and spine, killing within weeks. What time did I have left? Only God could save me.

I sat in a chair by my kitchen window, dazed and in shock. I found it difficult to think clearly, both because of the wild emotions and because of the painkillers I had been given earlier for my bone marrow biopsy. *Is my life over?*

I sat there, almost immobile, until Nick and David returned. My three boys fell on the kitchen floor, wailing and crying. Nick went into the living room to cry, not wanting to weep in front of the boys. I had never seen my family so sad and distraught. They were more devastated than I was. We'd had such a happy family, and we saw it all crumble under the weight of my diagnosis.

Then the first of many proofs of God's mercy came. We received a phone call from the oncologist.

David answered the phone. "Dr. Nayak," the oncologist said, "the initial report was incorrect. We reran the test. Your mother has acute lymphoblastic leukemia (ALL)."

My original assumption had been correct after all. Never in my life would I have considered a diagnosis of ALL good news. But in my case it was. Not as aggressive as the undifferentiated form, ALL is still a deadly, treacherous disease. But I had a little more time to find treatment and a fighting chance of beating it.

Nick and the boys got into action, researching the disease and treatment options. What a blessing to have so many doctors in the family! Or maybe it wasn't such a blessing. More than anyone, we knew the risks all too well. Fighting cancer is a battle, even for the more common kinds, such as breast cancer, which has 210,000 new cases a year, or lung cancer with 250,000. Only one thousand new adult cases of ALL are diagnosed each year. Most people who are diagnosed with ALL are under nine years old, so there are well-studied treatments for them. Those treatments do not work so well in adults. Since so few adults contract the disease, fewer studies have been done to determine what works and what doesn't.

And my prognosis? Only 50 percent survive the first year, and only half of them are still alive after five years. We were facing the real possibility that I wouldn't make it to Christmas.

One of at the first people I contacted was Smirit Parmer, who worked at MD Anderson Cancer Center in Houston. I had met her some years earlier in an airport before a flight to India. During the flight we became friends, sharing a common feeling about the plight of India's women. We stayed in touch, and I knew of her work in bone marrow transplant.

Immediately she said, "You get on a plane and come to Houston." She went on to describe the groundbreaking work the doctors there were doing for the treatment of ALL.

For some cancers, there are standard treatments, and most hospitals can deliver them effectively. In my case, there were only a handful of research centers with experience in treating adult ALL. Each one had its own protocols. The challenge was to choose the one that would give me the best chance at survival.

My ALL had been detected because of my high white blood cell count. What happens in leukemia is the bone marrow produces too many white blood cells. In ALL, the specific type of white blood cell that is overproduced is the lymphocyte. Normal bone marrow produces immature cells (also known as stem cells). Over time, the stem cells become either myeloid stem cells or lymphoid stem cells. The myeloid cells eventually mature into red blood cells, platelets, or granulocytes. The lymphoid cells mature into lymphoblasts, which further develop

CHAPTER 12: Making Decisions in a Whirlwind

into B lymphoblasts, T lymphoblasts, or natural killer cells (which go after cancer cells and viruses).

In acute lymphoblastic leukemia, too many stem cells become lymphoblasts, B lymphoblasts, or T lymphocysts. These cells do not fight infection well. They also crowd out the red blood cells, platelets, and healthy white blood cells. The results of this imbalance include anemia, infection, and easy bleeding. If not treated quickly, these cancer cells spread easily to the brain and spinal cord.

Many other types of cancer have staging systems, with stage 1 being the earliest and stage 4 indicating that it has spread widely. ALL has no such system. It's simply categorized as untreated, in remission, or recurrent because ALL is a disease of the blood. Once it is active, it's spreading. Other cancers start as contained tumors that grow in one place before spreading. Treatment of one small tumor is much different from treating multiple tumors in many parts of the body, so the staging system is helpful. Not so with ALL.

I had what is considered untreated ALL because my complete blood count was abnormal. A sample is considered abnormal if more than 5 percent of the cells in bone marrow are blast cells. My actual count was 80 percent.

Looking at the list of leukemia symptoms, I had the first: a feeling of being tired. I had always had an abundance of energy, so this feeling like I had a flat tire simply wasn't me. Nick's thought had been a simple anemia; mine, low thyroid. Neither of us thought I had anything more serious because as far as we knew, I had none of the risk factors for leukemia.

The risk factors for adult ALL include being male, white, and over seventy years of age. So far, I was zero for three. Other risk factors are prior chemotherapy, exposure to radiation from atomic bomb blasts, and genetic factors such as Down's syndrome. At first glance, I was now zero for six. But the last factor, the genetic one, was still an open question. Many adults with ALL have a genetic abnormality called the Philadelphia chromosome. If I was positive for the Philadelphia chromosome, then I had one of the risk factors for this disease. If that was the case, my prognosis was worse. Because I didn't have any of the risk factors that we knew of, ALL or other acute leukemias never entered our minds.

We spent the rest of the weekend reeling from the news, trying to adjust our thinking. Waiting for results isn't what I'm good at doing. I had to cling to God. All I could do was repeat words from the Psalms to myself over and over, reminding myself to remember God's promises.

Monday morning came—what used to be the start of a busy work week for me. Now my routine of exercise, devotions, and heading off to work had been cast aside. Zach phoned early in the morning. "Mom, last night I called one of my colleagues, a children's oncologist. I thought she might have some suggestions. This morning, I woke up to her voice mail. She said she knows someone at the University of Chicago. She went as far as to set up a phone appointment for you."

I called at the set time, and to my relief, Dr. Wendy Stock was very gracious with her time, speaking with me for an hour and answering my questions. She told me that I could receive the same kind of treatment at the University of Chicago that I would receive in Houston. Until that conversation, I was unaware of that possibility. That news gave me something else about which to think. I had been set to go to Houston, but it was so far away, and none of our family lived there.

At noon, the six of us went to church, where we prayed together. The elders laid hands on me and anointed me with oil. We felt so hopeless, so powerless. All we could do was trust God for the outcome.

As I prayed, I thanked God for the upcoming suffering, trying to be obedient to the command to give thanks in everything. I thanked Him that the suffering would bring me closer to Him and that He was preparing me for what I would need to endure. I asked Him to heal me and to reduce the pain that I would face, and that His will—not mine—be done. I didn't want to wallow in asking, "Why me?" I wanted to embrace God's will for me. Accepting His will was all I had to cling to, the only thought that gave me any sense of calm. At that moment, we needed wisdom for choosing a treatment center. I kept thinking of the good results MD Anderson had with ALL treatment.

CHAPTER 12: Making Decisions in a Whirlwind

When we finished praying, I raised my head and said, "Chicago." The word simply came out of my mouth. Like that, the decision was made.

I still had some doubts. Filling my brain were thoughts of a dear friend, Theresa, who had recently died of cancer. Before she passed, she told me she wished she had gone to Houston for treatment.

In the end, what swayed me were not statistics and protocols, but that fact that I would need my family around me during this journey. David and Alicia would be close at hand, as would Zach—at least until he graduated in May. Luke and Nick wouldn't be far and would be able to visit.

So Chicago would be the place of my journey.

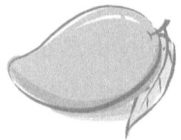

Chapter 13
Treatment Begins

When I started treatment, I had no idea how long the days would become, each one filled with its own trials and joys. Time stopped racing from week to month to year and crawled through each hour and minute. David filmed me making a video blog entry nearly every day. Much of what follows comes from those blog entries and e-mails Zach sent to family and friends.

We made arrangements for me to be admitted to the University of Chicago hospital in the afternoon of December 14, a Tuesday. I spent the morning packing, wondering if I would ever return to my home. No longer could I take it for granted that I would be given another day. So many emotions gyrated in my mind that it seemed I had lived a lifetime since Friday.

As I packed, I felt a certainty that I would never return to my house. Whatever treatments the doctors performed or drugs they administered, their efforts were simply a desperate try. I had no real hope anything would work.

One little miracle did give me some hope. I called my siblings over the weekend. My having cancer put into perspective the feud that had raged for sixteen years. Not only did I want peace and reconciliation,

CHAPTER 13: Treatment Begins

but I realized I needed my siblings in another way. At some point in my treatment, I would need a bone marrow transplant. The closer the match, the less likely my body would reject the transplant. Siblings are the best candidates for a full match. Zach calculated I had a 58 percent chance of finding an exact match among my three siblings. If siblings don't work out, the odds of finding a match plummet as the search widens through children, other relatives, and the bone marrow registry.

What I needed was for God to intervene so that my siblings would provide samples to see if they were matches. If any of them matched, then I needed their willingness to donate. My brother immediately provided blood samples to see if he was a match. I could only pray that my sisters would also be so inclined.

We left the house and went to the office to say goodbye to my employees. Some of them had been with me for over twenty years. Before we left the office, we sat in the conference room and filmed the first installment of my video blog, which we posted on a website we created called nayaksagainstleukemia.com. David started, introducing himself as Dr. David Nayak. He held himself together by being a clinician, trying to force back the feelings of a son. He summarized what had happened, what we knew so far, and the decision to seek treatment in Chicago.

Then Nick spoke a few moments about feeling like he had a hole in his heart because he knew the suffering I had ahead of me. Alicia cried as she spoke, speaking of what being part of our family had meant to her and that she could only trust God. Zach said, "When I am weak, He is strong." Luke made us laugh when he said we all knew the importance of family and that we would all rally around "the general." As I have said so many times, thank God for Luke!

Because of my family and their support, I could say to the camera, "I will be an eagle and not a turkey. I plan to use this time to get to know God better, to dwell in His presence and to be a strong witness for Him. I want to keep a positive attitude, to beat the cancer. Romans tells us to be joyful in all trials because they build character, which builds hope."

Still, it was with a sense of loss and foreboding that we set out from the office. We were leaving our known, happy, and healthy life to start the journey of cancer with its risks and suffering. As physicians, we thought we knew what lay ahead. In reality, we had no clue.

By early evening I was installed in the room that would be my home for the next month. David filmed a video tour of the room. I kept looking for the positive. I had room service, Wi-Fi, and space to set up a cot so Nick or one of the boys could spend the night. Getting settled in that room felt like setting up base camp for the climb to the top of Mount Everest.

A never-ending parade of doctors, nurses, and others came into the room. "Hi, my name is…" was their opening line, and they all had questions or a plan for me. In the next twenty-four hours, I would have a blood draw, a CT scan of my chest, a CT scan of my sinuses, a chest X-ray, a scan of my heart, and lines placed into my veins to allow for easy access to draw blood or give medications.

Among that parade was Dr. Wendy Stock, who was my principal oncologist. Her radiant and charming face immediately gave me a sense of relief and trust. I was surprised that she came to see me at eight o'clock at night and did not complain about the late hours or show any sign of fatigue or weariness. As I came to know her better over the next months and years, I would learn of her passionate devotion to her patients and how she always drew pictures as she talked, to show her patients what she was trying to explain to them.

Her first comment to me was, "You look very young and fit."

"Dr. Stock, I feel good and absolutely healthy."

Her face became grave as she told me, "Anjuli, you are going to be very, very sick. This chemotherapy regime we are starting you on tonight is an arduous process. You are going to lose your hair and suffer a lot. But in six months, you will recover."

Because of all the research my family and I had done over the weekend, none of her explanation was a surprise to me. Dr. Stock went on to inform me that this month, Dr. Andrew Artz was the attending physician, so I would see him every day. As my principal oncologist, she would follow my care closely. All of her statements gave me a sense of hope, confidence, and vision that I could beat this disease.

CHAPTER 13: Treatment Begins

On my blog, I said:

The big question right now is to determine if the cancer has spread to any other organ. The paramount concern is that it has spread to my brain or spinal cord. If that has happened, then my prognosis goes from being poor to much worse.

I know this is all for my benefit, but it's a little overwhelming. I'm used to being the doctor, the one in control, the one making and executing the plans. Now I'm just the pincushion to be poked and prodded at others' direction.

The next day, Wednesday, December 15, we got the genetics report back. It wasn't what I was hoping for. I had tested positive for the Philadelphia chromosome.

Sometimes bad news comes with a glimmer of hope. About seven years ago, having the Philadelphia chromosome was grim news for people with ALL. They simply didn't live as long as those without it. No one knew why; it merely was a fact. But over the last seven years, a new class of medications had been developed called tyrosine kinase inhibitors. When used with ALL patients with the Philadelphia chromosome, the results had been promising.

This news lit a spark of optimism. All of the mortality statistics at which we had looked were from people diagnosed before 2003. No one included in that group had received tyrosine kinase inhibitors. These new drugs haven't been out long enough or given to enough people to have a sufficient sample to study and from which to draw conclusions.

Dr. Stock was encouraging, almost happy about my being positive for the Philadelphia chromosome. Her thinking was that while the Philadelphia chromosome made my cancer more aggressive, the tyrosine kinase inhibitors would treat the effects of that genetic defect.

I was so grateful that she was my oncologist. She was the most compassionate doctor I had ever met. On top of her compassionate nature, she had trained under Dr. Janet Rowley, who had described the Philadelphia chromosome and had pioneered the research that has led to the treatment I was receiving. I knew I would not be able to find an oncologist better equipped to treat me.

My family and Dr. Stock discussed the treatment options. Two standard regimes have been developed for those with ALL and the Philadelphia chromosome, one for people under fifty years of age and one for those older. The older group receives less intense treatments because they are typically in poorer health and unable to handle the intense doses of chemotherapy that younger, healthier people can. Given my state of health and how I had been faithful and disciplined in exercise through the years, Dr. Stock agreed to use the more aggressive protocol. This one had a better chance of destroying all the cancer cells in my body.

The decision also impacted which tyrosine kinase inhibitor I would receive. The protocol for older patients used older tyrosine kinase inhibitors, which have been studied more. The protocol for younger patients used newer generation tyrosine kinase inhibitors, which are better at doing what they are supposed to do. So I would be receiving the newer generation drugs off-protocol. I was grateful for anything that gave me a better chance of beating this disease.

On my blog, I shared the latest news:

More diagnostic tests dominated the day, and so far, have brought good news. As far as the CT scans can show, the cancer hasn't spread anywhere in my body. I am grateful for that. I've had a migraine all day, due to the side effects of the chemo I'm receiving, but prayed it away. David has been with me, and I hurt to see him so shaken. He fights the tears as he describes how he feels like a bomb has been dropped on all of us. He's right, but our God will help us pick up the pieces and put them back, better than before.

Nick, David, and Luke are struggling with doubts, anxiety, and fear. They are coping with their distress by being clinicians, hiding behind medical terms that give them a little distance. Zach seems to have come the furthest in being able to just be my son. He says that hearing the first diagnosis, the acute undifferentiated leukemia, which is a more deadly disease than what I have, broke his heart. He's been forced to trust God, to face the sadness he will feel if I do not triumph in this battle, but he knows that God will comfort him. It appears he has found some measure of peace the other three have yet to find. I'm doing my best to encourage them all.

CHAPTER 13: Treatment Begins

I'm also encouraged by the number of people who want to come and visit me or send me cards, gifts, or flowers. Zach is serving as the communicator now, sending out regular e-mails and letting people know that I can't have flowers. Such beautiful things, yet they could be deadly to me. Once the chemo does its work, I'll have no immune system left, and the bacteria carried by flowers could give me an infection I won't be able to fight. I so much want visitors, but I know that once the chemo starts, I won't be able to be a gracious hostess when people come. Zach said the family will work out a way to manage visitors.

In other good news, my sister Manju agreed to be tested and to donate her bone marrow if she's a match, as Sudhir and Mridul did previously. I feel a little more secure, knowing that door is not completely shut.

By Thursday, Nick and the boys had my home away from home all set up. We brought my pink lamp from home and some plastic bins to hold my clothes. We taped a collage of pictures of family and friends to the bathroom door.

"Over the next four weeks," I recorded the following:

I'll be receiving chemotherapy that will kill all of the bone marrow cells in my body. This is where the cancer lurks, so first, what is there needs to be destroyed. Basically, they will be dripping poisons into my body. Today they inserted a PICC (peripherally inserted central catheter) line in my chest, right below my collarbone. They'll use this line to draw blood and give medications. While it's not fun to have this device implanted, it's far better than being stuck with a needle every time.

As I was reading the Scriptures this morning, I came across 2 Corinthians 4:7–12: "But we have this treasure in jars of clay to show that this all-surpassing power is from God and not from us. We are hard pressed on every side, but not crushed; perplexed, but not in despair; persecuted, but not abandoned; struck down, but not destroyed. We always carry around in our body the death of Jesus, so that the life of Jesus may also be revealed in our body. For we who are alive are always being given over to death for Jesus' sake, so that his life may be revealed in our mortal body. So then, death is at work in us, but life is at work in you."

That Scripture helped me ground myself and put on the full armor of God, defending me against doubt, fear, and anxiety. I told Nick and the boys not to focus on me but to focus on God. I found joy in trusting God, no matter what lay ahead. I was blessed to be able to share what God had done in my life with the recreational therapist, who came in to talk about the importance of exercise during my treatment.

Chemotherapy breaks down muscle mass, and exercise is the best way to build back up what the chemo destroys. So I set myself a goal. Since so few adults have ALL, many of us end up in research studies, as part of the ongoing effort to understand the disease and how to treat it. I recorded:

I'm going to do better than anyone else in the studies.

To do this, I'm committed to exercising as much as I am able. Earlier I did fifty minutes on the treadmill. I am now going to do the Thera-Bands, which is part of the exercise protocol. I read from the instructions: "Subject performs exercises three to four times a week over three to five weeks. Light stretching three to five minutes, bike or cycle five to ten minutes, resistance training five to fifteen minutes with dumbbells, bands, and exercise ball. Core exercises five to ten minutes." It's a demanding routine to follow, but I am determined.

The following day, Friday, December 17, I found myself quoting a poem I used to recite when I was five years old.

Lord, for tomorrow and its needs I do not pray

But keep me and guide me and love me, Lord, just for today.

Other Scriptures came to mind as well:

Come to me, all you who are weary and burdened, and I will give you rest. Take my yoke upon you and learn from me, for I am gentle and humble in heart, and you will find rest for your souls. For my yoke is easy and my burden is light (Matthew 11:28–30).

I wept as I read that passage. I wept because of the joy—because this was not my burden; it was His. I had tears running down my face as I experienced God's telling me to cast all my cares on Him.

Another Scripture God opened to me is John 10:10: "The thief comes only to steal and kill and destroy; I have come that they may

CHAPTER 13: Treatment Begins

have life, and have it to the full." I could feel the smile on my face as I repeated these words, knowing I was going to have life to the fullest.

In those early days, I counted my blessings: a good night's sleep, wonderful people around me, great nurses, support from my family. The steroids I had to take made me feel edgy and disturbed my sleep; at other times, my mood plummeted. But so far, praise God, these side effects were minor.

I was also grateful that the chemo and steroids hadn't affected me so much that I couldn't share what was going on with me and what God was teaching me. David came daily with the video camera and later posted what I said. This sharing gave me a feeling of connecting with the outside, with other people. Friends, relatives, my patients, professional colleagues, missionaries around the globe, anyone who heard of my illness was directed to my blog. We all felt this was the most efficient way to communicate with those who were concerned about my battle. At times, there were over seven thousand hits a day. It was such an encouragement when people posted comments or prayers.

That Friday, I had a lumbar puncture. In this procedure, some of the fluid that flows around the brain and spinal cord is extracted. The doctors can analyze the fluid to determine if the cancer has spread to my spine or brain. I was instructed to sit with my head bent toward my knees to make my spine curve outward, making the spaces between the vertebrae of my lower back bigger. That's where a needle was inserted. I was given local anesthesia, but it only dulled the pain. General anesthesia cannot be given for this procedure as the risks are too great.

I was prepared for the pain, but nothing prepared me for the popping sound the needle made when it entered my spine. The needle also touched a tendon, which really hurt. Afterward, I had to lie down for an hour because the draining of some of that fluid can cause severe headaches. It can also create herniation of the brain, which leads to immediate death. It was difficult not to think of these possibilities as I lay still, wondering if each little twinge was the start of something horrible.

As I lay there on my hospital bed, I tried to get my mind off myself and my pain. I realized that what I was going through was nothing compared to the pain Jesus endured for us as the big nails went through His hands. I was under anesthesia; He was not. I was hydrated; He was not. I was in a cool, air-conditioned room; where He was, it was hot. He was upright and exposed; I was comfortable, surrounded by the care of the doctors. When I thought about the nails that pierced His palms, all of my troubles and cares and pain faded away.

When I could get up again, I stuck to my resolution and went to exercise. I wheeled my IV stand with two bags of chemo hanging down, along with two pumps, to the exercise room, put on my mask, and got on the treadmill. While David filmed, I gave a little health lecture to my listeners about taking care of our bodies, eating healthy, and exercising. I told them that the less we become preoccupied with our ailments, the more we can see the goodness of God. I didn't want to sound like a preacher, but I believed this was all coming from the Lord. *He has blessed me with this journey, so that I can bless others,* I thought.

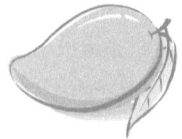

Chapter 14
Poisonous Honey

That Saturday morning I had early chemo and then unhooked my IV after seven days of being tethered to it. Oh, the little things that made me happy! I couldn't help doing a little dance, singing "Chick-a-boom-boom" as I walked to the bathroom. Now I could finally take a shower.

Nick and I went to the exercise room, and for about forty minutes, I walked the treadmill as he rode the stationary bike. Part of my energy came from Decadron, the steroid I was being administered, but I wasn't going to complain about that. It felt better to sweat out all of that energy anyway so I wouldn't feel so jittery and restless and could sleep. I had to wear a mask as I walked, ever mindful that I had no immune system left. Any little bug I picked up could be life-threatening.

It was Nick's birthday. "I'm sixty-two years old today," he said.

"No, no, you're sixty-one. You were born in 1949."

"By the Brahmin calendar and the tradition I grew up with, you are not aged by how many years you've completed, but by how many you've begun."

I walked a little on the treadmill before answering. "Since you are no longer in India and no longer a Brahmin, you should count by the

American calendar." I turned to look at him. "And could you please not tell the nursing staff you are almost sixty-five? "

"It's okay, Anjuli. I am not that young."

"But you are still tall, dark, and handsome, the man I married." I smiled at him. "I'd love it if you would wear colorful shirts every day when you come here to brighten my day."

He nodded and got off the bike. I finished my workout, got off the treadmill, and went to stand next to him.

"Nick, we had four legs before, but now we're a three-legged couple." I put my leg next to his.

At first he did not understand. "What do you mean?"

"Before, we were two interdependent people. Now we have to depend on each other. For the rest of our lives, we need to be intertwined, running on the same track. I want to enjoy your friendship during this time, to spend time with you—time we weren't able to spend when we were so caught up in the frenzy of our lives."

He looked into my eyes with sadness, but with a small measure of acceptance and surrender.

Later we got back the results from the lumbar puncture. There was no spread of the cancer to my brain or spinal cord. Those who wait on the Lord will have the wings of an eagle. I was flying high, deeply aware of how blessed I was that this disease had been caught so early.

That euphoria was short-lived, and it quickly turned into anxiety and deep depression. I wondered if I would ever be able to see my patients again, work as a physician, or interact with my colleagues and friends. I wondered if I would ever be able to travel again, to see the places I'd always wanted to visit. The thought of all this being stripped from me left me down and depressed.

Dr. Stock, hearing of my mental state, recommended that I meet with Dr. Tobin, a psychiatrist who specialized in helping cancer patients. The next day she walked into my hospital room: a slender, tall lady with deep-blue eyes who greeted me with a British accent. Immediately I recognized that she was an Irishwoman. She wanted to meet with me, one to one, alone for the next hour. I burst into tears as soon as Nick

CHAPTER 14: Poisonous Honey

and the nursing staff were gone, almost hysterical, venting to her about the great storm that had engulfed my life. She patiently listened to my story, not speaking much, only asking me about the nature of my mood and feelings. She had deep sympathy and concern for my emotional issues and reassured me that the inner turmoil I felt was normal. She also indicated that I was in a battle and should pursue wholeness, not only in my physical being but also in my emotional and spiritual health.

"Yes, Dr. Tobin, I understand this clearly. But I need your hand to get me through this."

She smiled. "It is a privilege to be here and to become a part of your story."

Feeling a tremendous sense of relief, I agreed to meet with her weekly.

In the meantime, we learned more from other test results. My white cell count had dropped considerably, well below normal levels, which was what we expected from the chemo. The goal was to eradicate all of the cancer cells in my body. In doing this, all of the normal blood cells would be destroyed as well. So even though my blood count was near zero, I had no blood cells and no platelets.

The Scriptures I read that Saturday told me that "outwardly we are wasting away, yet inwardly we are being renewed" (2 Corinthians 4:16). So true in my case. The old blood cells were being destroyed to make way for the new ones.

As my medical saga continued, Alicia acted the part of a great commander-in-chief. She arranged for home-cooked meals to be delivered at home for her, Nick, and the boys, and she saw to it that private-duty cancer nurses came to my room to help me around the clock.

I considered Alicia to be the daughter I never had. She understood my emotions and was very supportive of me. I hated to be addressed as a mother-in-law because of the negative connotation of that relationship all through my life, so I had made a conscious decision to receive Alicia as a God-given daughter, a new and welcome addition to our family. She and I had spent many happy hours shopping and going to spas together. She picked up little mannerisms in me and would laugh, "Oh, Mom Nayak, David is so much like you." I was determined not to repeat the pattern I'd seen in my mother's life in any way. David once commented that Alicia was closer to me than her own mother.

My three boys were so precious, spending time with me each day. Even in the midst of chemo, I was starting to realize what a blessing my illness was becoming to our family. We had all been going in different directions, pursuing careers and achievements, gathering awards and honors, but nothing is like the joy we know when we dwell together in the presence of the Almighty. I praised God for bringing us closer to each other and to Him, thankful for our common faith and the way we were all drawing together.

At the same time, the road ahead would not be easy. I knew I needed to trust God as I looked ahead to the treatment plan that had been worked up for me. I would be getting eight courses of intensive chemotherapy, each one lasting two weeks. That protocol would add up to nearly four months in the hospital. After that, the bone marrow transplant.

The next few days of videos recorded the early days of treatment.

Sunday, December 19

In a matter of a week, my immune system is down to zero. The steroids give me migraines, so I keep the lights dim. My body aches. I feel like a dead body lying in a bed, completely depleted. God gives me the strength to move. I'm battling through the nausea caused by the chemo, but I still was able to eat an entire small pizza.

I don't know how I would get through this without my family. I'm also grateful that the doctors and nurses are so gentle, kind, and compassionate.

I told Zach that I thank God for the gift of cancer. I see my suffering as an opportunity to grow closer to the Lord. Now I have time that I never had before to spend with the Lord in prayer, read Scriptures, and focus on him.

Luke will spend the night with me. It's such a comfort to have one of them with me. They're going to teach me how to use Skype so I can visit with people that way.

CHAPTER 14: Poisonous Honey

Tuesday, December 21

Yesterday was the roughest day so far. I'm coming off the steroids they gave me. The doses I was taking were about ten to fifteen times higher than the normal dose. It's making me so tired and giving me migraines. I'm still fighting the nausea, and I just don't want to eat. I was too tired to even try to record anything for the video blog.

I had a turbulent night, wrestling with nausea, dizziness, and vomiting that continued through much of the day. They come in waves, sometimes increasing in intensity, sometimes decreasing. I might feel good for a few minutes or an hour, and then a tsunami hits me, and I don't have enough energy to get out of bed.

This week I'll have an easier chemo regime, as they'll give me only one of the drugs from now until Sunday. I will still have the effects of the other in my system, and whatever side effects go along with it.

Eating is a struggle, so they have me on Ensure, which is loaded with calories and nutrients. I'm feeling so very weak. Only because of Jesus can I keep going.

I'm grateful for the Scriptures I've memorized in the past, as the words flow through my mind:

"LORD my God, I called to you for help and you healed me"
(Psalm 30:2).

"Jesus Christ is the same yesterday and today and forever"
(Hebrews 13:8).

"...I may dwell in the house of the LORD all the days of my life, to gaze upon the beauty of the LORD and to seek him in his temple. For in the day of trouble he will keep me safe in his dwelling; he will hide me I the shelter of his tabernacle and set me high upon a rock. Then my head will be exalted above the enemies who surround me" (Psalm 27:4-6).

I called out to the Lord, and He touched me with His angels. I had such a bad headache and nausea. He gave me strength to bear it.

Alicia came and read Scripture to me. I'm too weak to hold the Bible.

Wednesday, December 22

Today I had another lumbar puncture to check again for any spread of the cancer to my brain and spinal cord. While they were at it, they gave me some chemotherapy directly into those areas. The initial results were good, but I'll have to wait for the final results to come tomorrow.

The last twenty-four hours were the worst so far with the dizziness, nausea, and vomiting. I don't remember how many times I threw up, and this has left me frail and spent. I have barely been able to hold down liquids. The migraines are relentless. A lot of this is due to coming off the steroids, so Dr. Stock gave me a much smaller dose of steroids, and that seemed to help.

At some point during the day, I asked David if he still wanted to film me for the blog. He said, "No, Mom, you are too cute. We need you to get some rest."

By Thursday, December 23, an adjustment in my medications brought about a huge improvement. The migraines and vomiting decreased substantially. I finally was able to eat, and I ended up having two breakfasts that day.

David showed me the website with the video blog for the first time. It was fabulous. I felt so lifted up to see how everyone was praying. To my great delight, Nick had posted a prayer for me. Tears leaked from my eyes as I read:

> *I am praying to the Lord and saying,*
> "Hear me, LORD, and answer me,
> for I am poor and needy.
> Guard my life, for I am faithful to you;
> Save your servant who trusts in you.
> You are my God; have mercy on me, LORD,

CHAPTER 14: Poisonous Honey

for I call to you all day long.
Bring joy to your servant, Lord,
for I put my trust in you.
You, Lord, are forgiving and good,
Abounding in love to all who call to you.
Hear my prayer, Lord;
listen to my cry for mercy.
When I am in distress, I call to you,
because you answer me.
Among the gods there is none like you, Lord;
No deeds can compare with yours.
All the nations you have made
will come and worship before you, Lord;
they will bring glory to your name.
For you are great and do marvelous deeds;
you alone are God.
Teach me your way, Lord;
That I may rely on your faithfulness;
give me an undivided heart,
that I may fear your name.
I will praise you, Lord my God, with all my heart;
I will glorify your name forever.
For great is your love toward me;
you have delivered me from the depths,
from the realm of the dead.
Arrogant foes are attacking me, O God;
ruthless people are trying to kill me—
they have no regard for you.
But you, Lord, are a compassionate and gracious God,
slow to anger, abounding in love and faithfulness.
Turn to me and have mercy on me;
show your strength in behalf of your servant;
save me; because I serve you
just as my mother did.

Give me a sign of your goodness,
that my enemies may see it and be put to shame,
for you, LORD, have helped me and comforted me (Psalm 86).
I pray to God to make me an instrument to serve Anjee in good spirits and kindness.

Your loving husband,
Nick

I already felt better, more relaxed, just seeking the presence of the Lord. I read Nick's prayer again and again, feeling my heart fill with the joy of the unity Nick and I had—how he was experiencing my pain and turning it over to God. We truly were joined together in heart and spirit, something that had seemed impossible to achieve in India. One of the reasons I had wanted to flee was the sense that women could never have equality with men. Nick offered me this equality, something I had only dreamed about years ago.

Friday, December 24

Praise God, it's a much better day today. My headache has subsided, and I've stopped vomiting. I can read a little, even do a little exercise. Nick describes my condition as "being out of gas." He's exactly right.

I can read from the Bible and take comfort in reading: "'Because he loves me,' says the LORD, 'I will rescue him; I will protect him, for he acknowledges my name.'" (Psalm 91:14).

I feel like the wind has been blown out of my sails. They've taken me off the Decadron, so I feel limp and weak inside. Dr. Stock says my strength will come back. The way I feel now, I'm not sure I believe her.

I've been doing breathing exercises, and each time I take a breath I say, "Jehovah Rapha, Jesus the healer, come to me." He does come and suffers with me.

On Saturday, Christmas Day, I was still battling headaches, with a little nausea and vomiting, and I felt like a single thread trying to hold up a truck.

CHAPTER 14: Poisonous Honey

Fatigue wasn't a strong enough word for how I felt. Medications and ice packs helped a lot. The next day I would start another course of chemo, with high doses of steroids, so I expected these side effects to go away.

I received a wonderful Christmas present as well. The doctor gave me the good news that I wouldn't have to be in the hospital continuously for four months as I had thought. Sometime in January I would be able to leave for a week and then come back for more chemo. This news brought us all great joy. I was ready to leave my hospital room, which was beginning to feel like a prison cell. I wouldn't be able to go home to Bloomington, but just to be in a hotel would be a welcome change—even though all I would do was rest in between home health visits.

The rest of the family had Christmas dinner at Au Bon Pain on the first floor of the hospital. At the end of the day, as David was leaving my hospital room, I asked him to share one truth the Lord had shown him that day.

He took his time to answer the question, sitting down on the chair by my bed. He pulled his eyebrows together as he considered. After a long pause, he responded, "The Lord helps us to see good in tough situations." He was right. There was much good even in this situation. Our family was bonding in a way we hadn't for years, and we were leaning on each other, strengthening each other, drawing closer together.

I experienced another restless night, with nausea, vomiting, and headaches. In the morning I got another round of chemo and some new medicine for the nausea, which really helped. By afternoon, some of my appetite came back. I told David I wanted to eat so I would have the energy to walk on the treadmill.

"You're not going to want to do that," he said.

"I'll make it to the treadmill, you'll see," I replied. Shaking his head, he went to Au Bon Pain and ordered a turkey cranberry brie sandwich. Eating the sandwich and chips gave me some strength, enough to interest me in watching a little of the Bears beating the Jets 38–34.

A few hours later, I said to David, "I told you I'd make it to the treadmill today." With that, I put on my purple Nikes and walked to the exercise room. He followed me down the hall and talked with me as I worked out. I was supposed to wear a mask as I walked, just as a precaution against infection, but it got hot under there. David fussed like a mother hen, bugging me to keep the mask on. My energy level stayed high enough for me to even get a sponge bath.

That evening, my boys gave me the best present they ever could. They crowded around the bed, David and Zach each holding one of my hands, Luke with his hand on my shoulder. They whispered to me under the dim lights that this experience had brought them closer to the Lord. What a wonderful gift that was—more blessing in the midst of the pain!

Monday, December 27

I'm still dealing with headaches that come and go, but the medicines they've given me are controlling the pain. What little energy I have I need to save to speak to my family, doctors, and nurses, eat and exercise. The exercise is important because it stimulates the muscles that are weakened by the chemo, relieves the pain and stiffness in the joints, and keeps the blood circulating.

I was able to have a full breakfast this morning and do twenty-five minutes on the treadmill, fifteen minutes with exercise bands, and fifteen minutes of yoga. The best part was when I was on the treadmill because David read the Scriptures to me. His favorite parts were from Luke and Matthew when Jesus was healing people.

David came up with a great way to describe this whole process—my cancer, the chemotherapy, and the bone marrow transplant. What he says is the cancer I have is like a computer virus. My bone marrow is like the computer's hard drive. So I have a virus on my hard drive. The chemotherapy acts by erasing all of the information on the hard drive. After my hard drive (bone marrow) is erased and the virus (cancer) with it, we wait for the hard drive to reboot. The amount of time the rebooting takes varies from person to person.

Then following the analogy, just as a computer virus is wiped out when a hard drive is reformatted, sometimes it can come back. So one way to prevent this is to get a new hard drive. That's what the bone

CHAPTER 14: Poisonous Honey

marrow transplant will do for me, replacing my hard drive so I don't have a relapse.

For the transplant to be successful, the same type of hard drive is needed. This is why a full match is the best option.

Even I could hear how weak my voice was that day, but I still recorded a video blog, telling people this really was the best Christmas ever. We were praying that we were in God's will to rent a place here in Chicago so I wouldn't have to travel back and forth from Bloomington once I was released. I wished I could have visitors, but I agreed with the rest of the family that I needed to save my strength and not entertain people, as much as I wanted to see them.

On Tuesday, Dr. Artz noticed that my left arm with the PICC line was slightly swollen. I received chemotherapy, fluids, and other medications through that line. There was no redness, no pain, but it was a little enlarged. An imaging study was performed and a small clot was discovered at the tip of the PICC line. This occurrence was not unusual. The line was removed, and the clot was expected to dissolve on its own.

The timing was remarkable: I had received my last chemotherapy through that line and no longer needed it. The rest of my chemo would be done in pill form, at least until my doctors started the next round. What a blessing that the brilliant doctor spotted the swelling and caught this minor complication while it was still minor! Otherwise, the clot could have traveled to my lung, causing instant death.

Sometime during this first round of chemotherapy, I had a vision of the Lord. As much as I was able, I prayed and read my Bible. When I finished, I would zip my Bible in its cover and place it on the nightstand. One night around two in the morning, I felt I was rising from my bed. My body was lifeless; I felt that I was dead. I saw the waves of death swirling around me, torrents of destruction overwhelming me. I saw lightning through dark clouds and the Lord's approaching with smoke coming from His nostrils and fire coming from His mouth. He was shooting arrows, chasing away the death that was coming against me.

Suddenly there was light—bright light, and I woke up. I felt I had received life in me. My Bible was lying next to me, open to 2 Samuel

22:5–20. I had never in my life read this passage, and as my eyes passed over the words, I found myself reading a description of what I had just seen. I flipped over the pages of my Bible with shaking hands, my body in tremors, the hair standing up on my arms. My eyes landed on Psalm 18:4–19, a passage that is very similar, ending in the same way: "He rescued me because he delighted in me."

Wednesday, December 29

When David came into my room this morning, I greeted him with a smile and told him it would be a great day.

At the end of the day I was able to say, "This is my best day yet!" It's true. I'm eating every few hours and have my appetite back now that I have no nausea or headaches. I got on the treadmill twice. I also was able to take a shower since I'm unhooked from the PICC line. I'm so happy to have both hands free. I'm going to be cheerful with my two free hands! My blood counts are very low, which means the chemo is working.

One of the things I have learned is that I am going to ask in faith, nothing doubting. I don't want to be the double-minded man described in James, unstable in all of his ways.

Best of all, I had the energy to enjoy Nick's company. We've started writing love letters to each other. He loves to write, and I love to read his letters. When David was leaving for the night, I handed him a note to take to his father. "Don't peek," I told him. By way of answer, he gave me a broad smile with dimples, reminding me of the little boy he used to be.

Thursday, December 30

I'm feeling so much better than I did yesterday. Even though my blood counts are low, I'm feeling more strength and energy.

Today I read Psalm 19, verse 14. "May these words of my mouth and this meditation of my heart be pleasing in your sight, LORD, my Rock and my Redeemer." That's my prayer for today.

CHAPTER 14: Poisonous Honey

I claim the promise that God gave me about complete healing. I cherish every minute with my Lord, His presence, touch, and holiness. I am really enjoying the peace I have with Him. I want to start the new year seeking Him, walking on His holy ground.

I'm so grateful for those who watch my blog. I don't have the strength to see anybody, but I am encouraged that so many people are standing in the gap, praying for me. I can feel their prayers giving me peace. I don't know how this will end, but I have the assurance that all is well with my soul.

New Year's Eve arrived, more than two weeks into my journey of leukemia. God has truly been with me. As I lay in bed that night, unable to celebrate but strongly aware of the passage of time, I gave thanks to Him for the deep work He was doing in me. I was beginning to realize that my pride and arrogance—the pride I had felt in becoming a medical doctor, had created a trap around me. This trap had prevented me from truly being free in Christ. Through this journey, that trap was slowly being crushed.

I gave thanks to God for my doctors. Earlier in the day I saw Dr. Artz, who was so wise and discerning, so compassionate, with such a good bedside manner. I felt such empathy when he looked into my eyes. Who but God could send such a healer to me? He'd said I was doing well, that my body had responded to the poisons. I told him my body was responding to honey—honey that had killed the cancer cells, so it was sweet to me.

It had been days since I had nausea, vomiting, or headaches, so my appetite was back, and I was able to exercise. I was starting to lose little bits of my hair. A week or so before, Zach had shaved his head. He said he would continue to shave it so I wouldn't be the only bald one in the family. He also told me he was jealous of the time I had to spend with the Lord. I wanted to use the time I had to rest in Him. What else could I do?

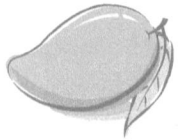

Chapter 15
Dashed Hopes

Saturday, January 1, 2011

My appetite is increasing, and I'm eating well. Six small meals today are giving me more strength. I did two thirty-minute sessions on the treadmill. No nausea, vomiting, or headaches. The one struggle I'm having is to be able to get to sleep. All of the steroids I've been on are giving me a "motor" that won't quit. That's not so bad since I'm able to exercise, but I could really use the rest.

As the new year began, my blood counts were recovering slowly as my "hard drive" rebooted. My prayer that New Year's Day was that I wouldn't contract any infections and that side effects would be minimal. More of my hair had fallen out. It covered my pillows, blankets, and pajamas.

I wasn't so bothered by the fact of my hair falling out. As a physician, I had long known that hair loss follows chemotherapy like winter follows the fall. Nick reassured me over and over he loved me, with or without hair. What bothered me was how irritating it was that the hairs somehow made their way into my eyes, nose, and mouth. I couldn't seem to get free of them. Even after I thought I had removed them all, I could still feel the itchy prickling.

CHAPTER 15: Dashed Hopes

I saw Dr. Larson, the head of the oncology and hematology service, that morning. All of the doctors took turns seeing the patients on weekends, coming to their rooms. He was a kindhearted man, very distinguished-looking. He shocked me when he congratulated me on surviving the chemotherapy and said, "Hopefully, we can translate this to a cure. You are a great, healthy candidate for it. Your white count is going up; your hemoglobin is going up." He looked deeply into my eyes and slowly nodded his head.

I struggled to process what he was saying. Before this, I hadn't really imagined that I had hope. Even with the vision I'd had from the Lord and my determination to stand in faith, I had still been discouraged, believing that surviving acute lymphoblastic leukemia was nothing more than a fantasy. I wasn't sure if the vision had meant I'd be cured or that God would take me to heaven. With just a few words delivered in a calm, almost stoic manner, Dr. Larson had reassured me. "You're the kind of patient we like to have," he said.

Trying to hold back tears, I reached for a tissue from the box on my bedside table. "Dr. Larson, as a colleague and a fellow physician, I am humbled to be here. I have never been sick in my life, and I am vulnerable today in a fashion I never have been before. I have come to the best place, the University of Chicago. Tell me your thoughts and where I go from here. What would you do if you were in my position?"

He thought for a moment. "I would do the same as you."

"Do I have a chance?" I held my breath, hoping he would confirm what I thought he was telling me.

"Yes, you do have a chance."

I leaned forward. "I am not a patient. I am a conqueror, a survivor. I want to live for a better outcome for my patients and my family. I will stick with every piece of advice you give me, and with God's grace and mercy." Grace and mercy had already been there for me in ways I had never before experienced, and I knew it would continue.

After that conversion, I grew much quieter inwardly and could feed on the Word of God to a whole new degree. My friends, Bob and Sandy, visited and laid hands on me, praying and worshiping with me, thanking

God for His miracles. I felt that I had been redeemed, pulled from the jaws of death. Their prayers helped me feel surrounded by God's angels ministering to me. My mind was not racing the way it was only twelve hours earlier.

That evening I lay resting in my bed. Nick was curled up on the cot, snoring quietly. Earlier he had bathed me. He had me sit on a little stool and fussed over the temperature of the water. He kept telling me not to move as he applied the soap and voiced dismay when more of my hair fell out. His painstaking efforts told me he was a little nervous, doing something he'd never before done. But he was gentle, and I love the gentle touch of Nick.

As I fell asleep, I asked God for special grace for my family and rest for their souls as they gave so much out in supporting me.

Sunday, January 2

I'm stronger today. I've already walked on the treadmill for forty-five minutes, done my bands. My hair is going, thinning. It's all over the bed, black strands twisted into the pillow and wrapped up in the sheets.

I am resting in the arms of the Almighty. I'm not getting much rest otherwise, which is a continuing side effect of the steroids. I'm also feeling moody and irritable. Sometimes I don't care about the results; I just want this suffering to end.

My body is weak, but my heart is strong in the Lord. I continue to be sustained by the grace of God. Later I may even watch the Bears game. The big joy in that is that I'll be able to watch it at a hotel, as I was discharged today. Praise God for that!

I thought I would feel so much better out of the hospital, but as Monday dawned, I felt terribly anxious and nervous. I knew my emotions were side effects of the medications, but that knowledge really didn't help much. I also hated seeing clumps of dark hair falling from my head every time I touched it.

David told me that I should not let the cancer dictate when I would

CHAPTER 15: Dashed Hopes

lose my hair. "Let's do it on our terms!"

He went out and bought a pair of clippers and went to work. When he was finished, he presented me with a red UnderArmour skull cap. That gift brought a smile to my face and a little calm to my soul.

When Nick saw my bald head, he said, "Your head is perfectly round. You look so beautiful and are an exact replica of your father."

Tears rolled down my face. I was worried that my femininity was lost when my head was shaved, and that Nick would no longer find me attractive. That he compared me to my very good-looking father reassured me better than any other words he could have chosen. I stood to hug him, clinging to the man who was a tower of support and love for me.

Tuesday, January 4

It's a much better day, getting back into the swing of the new year. I've been on the treadmill for thirty minutes, and I watched the news and got caught up with what's going on in the political realm.

Everything that's been happening has been a blessing, and I'm determined to beat this disease. My family has rallied around me, and I'm so grateful. My bandana looks fabulous—much better than scraggly, falling-out hair.

On Wednesday, January 5, I had a pulmonary function test to assess how my lungs were doing. For so many years, I had been the one ordering this kind of test for my patients. The experience gave me a new perspective to be the investigational subject sitting in the big box blowing into a tube. I was not surprised to be able to perform all of the instructions correctly.

David asked me about my hair. I told him that whatever was between my ears was getting stronger and better without it and that I felt excellent. He and Alicia were caring for me and Nick very well.

The next day, I would go back to the clinic to do more investigations after I got on the treadmill. I was pleased that the whole time I'd been at the clinic that day. I had had the strength to walk and didn't need the wheelchair. The exercise was paying off.

Friday, January 7

It's been exactly four weeks since my diagnosis, and I'm grateful the medical help came to my assistance right away. Otherwise, I'd probably be in my grave by now.

Every prayer has been answered, and I feel so much better. I'm exercising, getting better nutrition, feeling stronger. Whatever happens with my life is not that important; every day I see prayers answered.

It seems like I haven't slept for weeks and weeks. Sometimes the anxiety gets to me. The only way to fight it is to think about what's good in this situation—like how I am enjoying my kids: Luke, Zachary, David, and Alicia, and how they have rallied together.

Or how I can rest in the promise that when God is with me, who can be against me, and that the peace of God will occupy our hearts and minds.

If it wasn't for the prayers of the saints, I would not have seen this day. I wouldn't have been able to survive this. I can't thank those who pray for me enough.

Saturday, January 8

I pray that there will be harmony among my family members. All of them have their hearts in the right place. This is a team effort—all of the Nayaks against this cancer: Nick, Luke, Zach, David, and Alicia.

But the anxiety and the stress are getting to them. There's conflict among them; I can sense it. They are hiding it from me, so as not to worry me. It's hard not knowing what's going on. I pray that they will be protected against the schemes of the Enemy.

That Sunday, I was able to watch church services on the Internet and eat lunch with the whole family. The sermon told me that no matter what I was going through in life, I was not alone. There is a lot of darkness and depression, but there is help. This cancer of mine would be healed. When we cry out, God listens to us. He prepares us for His purpose. God wanted me here to experience His sovereignty, and He would give me the grace to endure. Hard times would be there, but God would never depart from me. He would never leave me nor forsake me.

CHAPTER 15: Dashed Hopes

With all of the ups and downs of chemo, medication, and change, I had cried out so hard in the past month, and God had heard my cry of desperation. I reminded myself, *He has gotten me this far. My soul is completely sold out to the Lord. I am willing to submit. I want to know that my expectation is from the Lord, and these hard times will go away.*

In all of this, what matters is that God be glorified at my expense. I also know that God's way is the best way. His way is perfect, and His promises are there for me. He is like a gardener, pruning me, taking all of the little twigs and dead wood out of the way so that the fruit will be juicier and more useful for His kingdom.

I clung to the words of Psalm 37, verses 3 and 4:

Trust in the Lord and do good;
Dwell in the land and enjoy safe pasture.
Take delight in the Lord,
And He will give you the desires of your heart.

Monday, January 10

Lots of good news today. The results of my bone marrow biopsy show that I am responding well to the chemotherapy and am in hematological remission. This means they cannot detect any cancer cells in my bone marrow. I'm feeling much better; the side effects are gone, and I'm sleeping well.

Today, Psalm 139:1, 16 has been on my mind. So much in it relates to what I am going through: "You have searched me, LORD, and you know me. Your eyes saw my unformed body; all the days ordained for me were written in your book before one of them came to be."

Everything that we go through in this life is ordained, and God knows the blueprint. We simply need to trust Him and pray to Him to search us, to test us, to know our anxious thoughts.

On Wednesday I moved back to the hospital for my next round of chemotherapy. This regimen would be less intense than the first, but it would still be poison dripped into my veins. Like the first round, part would be given through the IV and part in pill form.

Before the chemo was started, a central port was placed into my chest. This replaced the PICC line, giving a permanent access to administer drugs and draw blood.

During our stay in the hotel, Zach commented that it was strange to be on the other side—to be the patient rather than the physician. He paced around the pale green room, pausing at the window to look at Lake Michigan. "It's disempowering, in that the control we are used to having has been wrestled away. What we eat, when we sleep, where we sleep, and the physical boundaries of our bodies are violated."

I could empathize. As doctors, we constantly ask people personal details of their lives or probe intimate places in their bodies. It was difficult for Zach to watch all of this done to me, his mother, not just any patient. But as tough as it was, I knew this experience was enlightening for him and would make him a better doctor. I thought back to my experiences as a med student, where the patients in the STD clinic had to disrobe on the veranda, completely disregarding any sense of privacy. I had taken that for granted. After practicing medicine in America, I quickly came to see the lack of privacy as violation of their human dignity, and my new faith likewise showed me the value of every human being. Now my ordeal was giving me a more personal sense of dignity and privacy, and Zach was learning this lesson alongside of me. He would be sure to respect the dignity of all his patients after this.

After the central port was in place, Zach told me it was quite disturbing to see me with a foreign object placed in my chest, bulging slightly. He had seen the procedure done many times before, but it had an emotional impact when it happened to his own mother. He hurt to see me like this, and my heart ached for him. I knew the burden he had for me and how it weighed him down.

Since that procedure went smoothly, my intravenous chemo was started. I continued to be able to get on the treadmill, even though I was hooked up to the IV stand that I had nicknamed "my dancing partner, Skinny Dr. Nick."

Two things I prayed for that night: fewer side effects of the chemo and a bone marrow match. Finding the second would be like searching the entire city of Chicago for one specific brick.

CHAPTER 15: Dashed Hopes

Thursday, January 13

After breakfast, I put in sixty-five minutes on the treadmill, with Skinny Dr. Nick pumping chemo into me. Then I was off for a lumbar puncture, with chemo administered to the brain.

So far, no headaches and few other side effects. I even felt well enough to eat and enjoy a Big Mac. My doctors are very pleased with my progress, and the exercise gives me energy. I hope that I can go through this regimen with courage and perseverance.

The international bone marrow registry with its ten million or so registered donors did not come up with a match for me. All three of my siblings have sent blood and mouth swabs for analysis. We are praying that one of them will be a full match.

Friday, January 14

I have blisters on my feet, so I couldn't walk on the treadmill today. I did forty-five minutes on the stationary bike instead. The chemo continued throughout the day. To pass the time, Nick and I enjoyed a few card games.

I have a sense of helplessness, but our God is all-powerful. There are waves of nausea and side effects, dejection and anxiety, followed by other waves of relief and hope. God is my strength, whatever wave is washing over me.

That Sunday, January 16, I went from a mountaintop to another valley. First, the mountaintop: I was discharged from the hospital on Saturday because the chemo I was getting through the IV had been finished earlier in this stay. My counts would continue to drop as I continued taking chemo in pill form, and I would get weaker and be more susceptible to infection. The risk of getting an infection in the hospital was much greater. So we had the joy of leaving. Then we plunged into the valley. At two in the morning, I had a fever of 101.3°. A person with a normal immune system can fight off that fever. I couldn't. And fevers are often the only sign of infection. Since a fever that high could be life-threatening to someone in my condition, my family took me into the emergency room. After a few hours, the doctors decided I didn't have an infection and sent me home.

Monday, January 17

My fever is gone, and I'm not feeling any of the side effects of chemotherapy. I'm feeling so much better, able to notice the snow outside, to reflect on Martin Luther King Day.

These words from James 1 take on new meaning for me: "Consider it pure joy, my brothers and sisters, whenever you face trials of many kinds, because you know that the testing of your faith produces perseverance. Let perseverance finish its work so that you may be mature and complete, not lacking anything."

I am looking forward to the day of my redemption. My faith is getting stronger and stronger. I am so blessed that I had this diagnosis, that I could experience the joy, peace, calmness in my inner soul because I am grounded in His Word.

We got the news today that two of my siblings, Sudhir and Mridul, are half-matches. Basically, there are four markers doctors look for when trying to determine a match. All four have to be identical for a perfect match. A half-match isn't good enough. When two of the four markers don't match, it's likely the recipient will reject the transplanted bone marrow.

Sudhir and Mridul have done all they can to help. Sudhir organized a bone marrow donation drive in Bloomington, and Mridul did the same in Dayton. She also took advantage of a family wedding in India of a relative on our father's side to have mouth swabs collected from all of the relatives in attendance. She then arranged for those swabs to be flown to a lab in Atlanta for analysis. Sadly, none of this effort turned up the full match for which we were looking.

We continue to pray. There is still Manju. Of course, even if the tests determine that she is a full match, all that means is she's passed the screening test. They'll do further, more intensive testing on her blood sample to make sure she is a full match. We'll have to wait a few more days for those results.

Tuesday, January 18

Today I had my fourth lumbar puncture, and they administered the chemo to my brain and spine. So far no complications. I was able to get on the treadmill and spend time with Nick.

Thanks be to God, who always leads us ... in Christ's triumphant procession! (2 Corinthians 2:14).

Nothing has sustained me as much as the realization that Jesus is always present with me. This realization is independent of my feelings, worthiness, or perceptions of how Jesus should demonstrate His presence toward me. God wins His greatest victories through apparent defeats. Very often the Enemy appears to triumph, just for a season. God allows it. Then He comes in and upsets the work of the Enemy, saying, "Go away, Satan." Consequently, God then gives us a much greater victory than we would have ever known.

I think of the story of the three young men thrown into the fiery furnace. We've all been in such situations where we think we are defeated. In that situation, the enemy was astounded to see them walking around in the fire, enjoying themselves. This apparent defeat was turned into a victory.

That's what I am seeing. From the time of my diagnosis, the Enemy has not taken a stronghold in me. So I am not acknowledging defeat. No defeat for me! I claim the victory through our Lord Jesus Christ. I tell my doctors I am not a patient. I am an overcomer and a conqueror in Christ Jesus.

Wednesday, January 19

I feel the best I have in a long time because I got to take a shower after one week of being hooked up to the IV! Thank God for being able to follow my daily routine. The exercise and healthy eating help, but I know it is the prayers of the faithful who have brought me this far.

I'm going to deal with this head-on. God is Jehovah Raphah, the Healer.

Thursday, January 20

Over and over I repeat to myself the verse from the Psalms: "I was overcome by distress and sorrow, Then I called on the name of the LORD" (Psalm 116:3b, 4a). I called out to God, and he heard me. I have seen this fulfilled in a miracle. My older sister, Manju, is a full match! She has agreed with love and joy to come and donate.

I have to remind myself this is only the first step. There are a lot of unknowns—of what will transpire now, of how the doctors will use this.

God has sustained me and given me courage, hope, and a bright smile. I want to serve the Lord with a renewed spirit—in ways I have never before experienced. Life is not the same after a diagnosis of cancer. I want to use what life I have in better ways.

Saturday, January 22

Some days, like today, I feel weak, unable to move, like someone let the air out of my tires. In spite of it, I'm able to muster up courage and strength, because I do not want to dwell in fear, anger, depression and restlessness. I just want to dwell at Jesus' feet.

My heart continued to change day by day. When I got the diagnosis, my first response was to have a party—a pity party. But I did not do that. I trusted in God. He responded by doing some healing in me. A sense of restoration, of renewal filled me even as the days passed in treatments and doctor visits. My doctors continued to be among my greatest blessings, especially Dr. Tobin, who helped me see what hope remained no matter how my emotions sometimes raged.

I knew the Lord would help me face whatever was still ahead: the bone marrow transplant, the possibility of infection. I prayed for my older sister, who would be coming here soon. She didn't normally keep in good health, and I asked God to make this all easier for her.

By Friday, January 28, my overwhelming feeling was one of tranquility, even though I was weak inside because of all of the chemotherapy. My brain was clear and my cognitive skills sharp. I was able to read a lot of clinical articles, as well as the Word of God. He

CHAPTER 15: Dashed Hopes

continued to reveal much to me. My blood counts were doing well, and I was able to do forty minutes on the bike, thirty minutes of treadmill, and forty minutes of yoga. My stamina was improving, which would help me endure the transplant. I played cards with my children, and Nick teased me that I beat them every time.

Truly, every day at that point was a brand-new day. I thanked my Father for the time He gave me, and for the relationship I was cultivating with Him that I couldn't have had with the busy life I was running. I felt so blessed by my loving, supportive husband, and by my sons and daughter-in-law. When Alicia came to visit me, it was like a sunflower's opening; she brought so much joy to my heart.

But by the end of that Friday, my serenity and trust were shaken. I huddled in my thick white bathrobe, protecting myself from the cold and the harsh reality of the news I was trying to accept. Because of some medical issues of her own, Manju would not be able to be the bone marrow donor.

Now what?

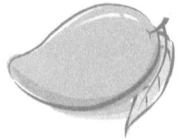

Chapter 16

Exploring Options

Saturday, January 29

Once again, I am solely dependent on God as to what is going to happen. As the saying goes, when God closes a door, He always opens up a window.

Feeling desperate after the news about Manju, I returned for another of my regular sessions with Dr. Tobin. Sitting in her tiny office that barely had room for two chairs, I cried out to her. "Dr. Tobin, I am so discouraged by the strikes that are coming against me."

"I understand, Dr. Nayak." She leaned forward and put her hand on my shoulder. "So have patience and courage, and do not give up hope. You are in the best of hands. Dr. Stock will do her utmost to give you a new life."

With the possibility of a full match most likely gone, we continued to think about our options. The chemo was doing its job for now, and once I was in complete remission, we could move to the next phase of the journey—whatever that might be. The possibilities were to:

1. Continue with chemotherapy
2. Transplant unrelated full-match stem cells

CHAPTER 16: Exploring Options

3. Transplant unrelated umbilical cord blood cells
4. Transplant half-related stem cells

We planned to meet with Dr. Stock the next week to talk about the benefits and risks of each option. The second one gave the best chance for recovery, but since none of my siblings had worked out as a donor, it was unlikely we could do it. An unrelated full-match donor would have to be of Indian origin, probably from northern India. There weren't many Indians listed in the bone marrow registry in America and Europe, and there is no national registry in India. Nick and our relatives were trying to register new donors, but the chances of finding a full match were small.

By this time, we had settled into a two-bedroom furnished apartment in Chicago, giving us a home base for the duration of my treatment. The noise of ambulances and police sirens disturbed our peace at all hours of the day and night, but from our perch on the fourteenth floor, I felt we had created a little oasis where we could retreat from the bustle of the city. Though no pictures hung on the beige walls, it was beginning to feel more like home. I resumed cooking, making breakfast for Zach early in the week and a meal for my family one day. It was a small thing, but just one more reminder of the life I had once taken for granted.

As the week wore on, I started to notice some pain in my eyes—dryness, itchiness, and redness. It got worse until I couldn't even face any light. So it was back to the emergency room.

I was told I had inflammation in my eyes. I'd been taking eye drops to prevent complications that one of my chemotherapy drugs could cause. We continued them longer than we should have, and when we learned it was time to stop, we did. What we didn't know was that I was supposed to have done a slow withdrawal, not an abrupt stop.

This miscommunication led to my eye pain, but thankfully the ER had the right medication to correct it. As a physician, I know how often this happens in the medical world. It's so hard to communicate all the details in a way that patients and their families can comprehend. Complicating the process is that when people are sick and emotionally stressed, it's harder for them to understand and to remember all of the instructions they're given. Praise God, in my case, we were able to see a specialist before any lasting harm was done.

As January drew to a close, Chicago was awaiting a big snowstorm—one the news was calling "the blizzard of the century." With twenty-four inches of snow expected, the city would be closed. Great fear was instilled in the residents of Chicago and central Illinois. As I listened to the news, I could only think, *but we do not need to fear because we have a God Who will protect us.* We needed to be proactive, of course, and get our milk and bread, but the storm was going to come and go—just like the storm of cancer in my life.

As I sat there watching the forecast, I allowed myself to recognize what I felt: that the cancer had left my body. I would have another bone marrow test to see if I was in remission and discuss my options. I prayed that I would feel no fear, that I would be strong, and that whatever my doctor said we needed to do, my body would be able to take it. Day by day, step by step, I would get to a cure. *I am not a patient; I am a conqueror in Christ Jesus.*

Over the next two days, everything in Chicago closed down because of the snow. Lake Shore Drive, the transportation network—everything—but Alicia had to go to work anyway. The mayor did not call to tell his employees to stay home. My doctor's appointment, of course, was postponed.

This delay was hard for me because I continued to battle anxiety. I knew that God could calm my fears, but as Zach told me, this knowledge required that I actually turn my anxieties over to the Lord. It was another little bit of control I needed to surrender. Dr. Tobin had been helping me consider my need for control like a demon that harassed me, and that when I lost control, my anxiety escalated. Turning my life over to God, giving the control over to Him, helped defeat the demon and reduce my agitation.

On Wednesday, I had a little difficulty breathing due to bronchitis. The allergist in me prescribed a breathing treatment. Someone from the family went and got a nebulizer. I looked at it and asked, "How do you work this thing?" We all laughed over that comment—that

CHAPTER 16: Exploring Options

after twenty-five years as an allergist, I didn't know how to put the nebulizer together. My wonderful staff had done that for me for so long, I'd forgotten how!

We got the nebulizer assembled, and I sat for the treatment. In a word, it was boring. Halfway through, I decided to lie down. What an irony for this allergist, who has prescribed thousands of these treatments, to be subjected to the same dull twenty minutes and the rapid heartbeat and muscle twitching the medicine caused!

I did not sign up for this cancer. Yet I consider this whole cancer deal worth it if in the end I look more like Jesus and sound like Him. I want it to be obvious that I have spent time with Him. It's worth it if somehow I can honor Jesus by going through this experience, whatever the outcome.

So I'm asking Jesus to make it worth it. I want to be more like Him. I want to see my illness from Jesus' perspective. There's a lot that I don't understand, but I'm trusting Him.

I can't sometimes see down the road. But I'm still grateful that Jesus knows the beginning to the end and everything in between for me.

Even on days that I am holding on to Jesus, I realize it is Jesus' grip that is keeping me together. I thank Him for His unmistakable grace.

On Thursday, Dr. Stock saw me in the clinic. When she walked into the room, I fired questions at her. "What's next for my treatment? When will I feel completely normal? How many weeks? How many more rounds of chemotherapy? How many more spinal taps? Bone marrow biopsies?" In my impatience, I didn't even give her time to answer one question before I asked another.

She laughed. "You're feisty today." It was true. I was feeling a little more like my old self.

She sat down at the wooden desk across from the examination table and drew an overall road map of what was to come. I leaned across the desk, following every stroke of her pen. "Remember," she said, "all this hangs on the results of your bone marrow biopsy next week. Only then will we know where we stand and can put together a more definite plan."

I thought carefully about what she said next: "With cancer, things can change very quickly." That was true. There's also lots of waiting—waiting for test results, waiting to see if side effects will come or if they will go.

Sunday, February 6

Yesterday, we celebrated Luke's eighteenth birthday at Shang Hai Terrace, one of my favorite restaurants. I always associate chicken corn soup with birthdays, ever since I started celebrating mine at Chung Fa in India. Even though the soup tastes exactly the same, the contrast of the décor of those two restaurants is worlds apart. Torn plastic covers covered Chung Fa's booths, and greasy splatter marks decorated the walls, while noodles stuck in the air-conditioning window units bobbed up and down, blown around by the air forced outward from the rattling machines. At Shang Hai Terrace, elegant Chinese art hangs on the walls, surrounding a room furnished with intricately carved rosewood chairs and a view of a terraced rose garden. As far as the air conditioning at Shang Hai Terrace, it functions invisibly and inaudibly to the patrons, so if noodles are dangling in it, I have no clue.

For a few hours, I didn't feel like I have cancer. This is a rare feeling for me these days. I know that life will never be the same again, almost as if I've had a limb amputated. I'll regain some functioning, maybe almost all of it, but not the way it used to be.

Today I'm feeling rather weak. Because of my low red cell counts, it takes a lot of energy merely to do the simple tasks. The weakness is making me feel low. A few weeks ago I told my boys I want to live to see Luke graduate from high school and Zach from medical school. Today I'm not so sure I'll make it.

Nick asked a good question. How can a good God let something bad happen? Zach's answer is that God Himself is not immune to suffering. In the person of Jesus Christ, He endured much suffering on our behalf.

CHAPTER 16: Exploring Options

Monday, February 7

I had the bone marrow biopsy today and am a little sore. I am praying that the results will show that I am in complete remission and can proceed with the bone marrow transplant. It's a difficult road ahead, but I am certain that I will come out victorious.

I had a new revelation from the Bible. In Matthew 17:20, it says nothing will be impossible for you. So it's possible for me to cast all my anxieties on Him and accept my circumstances with singing instead of complaining.

I was a little disappointed when the Packers beat the Bears, but they deserved the victory. They are a great team and fought hard for the win. May God grant victory to my team as we fight my cancer.

Wednesday, February 9

Today I got word that I am in morphological remission. This means that the cancer cells have responded to the chemotherapy—in other words, they are gone. I can say with confidence, Hallelujah! No more cancer cells are in my body!

God has been good to me from Day 1. I am so grateful for this news. The next step is the bone marrow transplant, which will be an uphill battle. I rest in the shadow of the Almighty.

In this journey I have turned from turmoil to peace, from anxiety to trust, from worry to assurance. If only I could stay peaceful, trusting, and assured all of the time!

The day after learning I was in remission, I was energized enough to write a letter to the children in an orphanage in India that Nick and I had supported for many years.

Hello to all of you, my children!

I am writing to tell you that I love your e-mails and prayers! I know that God hears the prayers from all of you, and I feel all of them. I am so grateful for your prayers—the prayers of the saints! I love each of you very much!

I want you to keep up with your studies, both at school and in the Bible. God has such wonderful plans for each of you! I am so happy that I can witness God's love and His work in each of your lives. Maybe one of you will go to university to become a doctor or a scientist and develop the cure for cancer!

I am on a long, tough journey. But I am not alone in this journey; I have Jesus Christ. I am comforted by this Scripture: "I will lead the blind by ways they have not known, along unfamiliar paths I will guide them; I will turn the darkness into light before them and make the rough places smooth. These are the things I will do; I will not forsake them" (Isaiah 42:16). I am leaning on Him, trusting in Him, and I am turning all of my anxiety and cares to Him (Philippians 4:6: "Do not be anxious about anything, but in every situation, by prayer and petition, with thanksgiving, present your request to God").

I am glad to be on this journey. I am growing closer to Christ and suffering as He suffered for me, for us, for all of us and our sins! This is not a journey I would have chosen, but I humbly accept this cup as Christ has done before me. Psalm 16:5: "Lord, you alone are my portion and my cup; you make my lot secure."

Please pray for me. Pray for protection from the Enemy, that my faith will not fail. Please pray for my family, as this is a hard time for them as well.

Most of all, remember Mark 12:30: "Love the Lord your God with all your heart and with all your soul and with all your mind and with all your strength." Christ's love for us is so great we can't understand it completely! I feel God's love, and I love Him with all of my being. Especially at this time in my life, I am even more cognizant of this!

Please keep your letters, e-mails, and prayers coming! I enjoy them immensely! Thank you, and I love each one of you very much!

Love,
Aunty Dr. Anjuli

CHAPTER 16: Exploring Options

A follow-up with the eye doctor revealed no lasting damage to my eyes. I got some nice workout clothes so I wouldn't have to exercise in my pajamas, and I also got a wig, so I was no longer limited to scarves or showing off my bald head. These little measures added to my comfort and helped me along this journey. But they paled in comparison to what happened that Friday: I got to see my brother and sisters! I hadn't seen my two sisters in fifteen years, and I was so happy that I could see Sudhir and his wife, Indira, along with Manju, Mridul, and her husband, Anil.

They came to the apartment, arriving together. David opened the door for them, and as they entered, I pulled off my wig and shouted, "Yoo-hoo!" There was a big laugh at that. After a lot of hugs and tears, we crowded into the small living room and found seats on the sofa, the daybed, and the recliner. My sisters sat near me on the daybed. Nick offered them masks as part of our infection-control regime. They all solemnly took a mask and put it on. In keeping with Indian tradition, Nick scurried around preparing chai, serving everyone.

"You look so good, even with no hair," Mridul commented. "We were imagining a scrawny skeleton of an Anju."

"Have you been juicing?" Manju asked. I took her into the kitchen to show her the contents of my refrigerator, stocked with broccoli, kale, green apples, carrots, and celery. "Good, Anju. How much protein do you take in a day?" She leaned against the black granite countertop and looked into my face.

"Three boiled egg whites."

"Do you eat lentils or beans?" These were not unexpected questions from my vegetarian sister.

"I don't need them. I eat beef, chicken and fish."

She started at me blankly, with puzzled eyes. "Are you eating organic?"

"All my produce is from Trader Joe's." I didn't take offense at her questions. I knew nutrition was important to her, and this was her way of expressing her concern for me.

After about an hour of chitchat and watching some amusing videos of Mridul and her husband dressed up in traditional Indian garb, dancing like Bollywood stars, we all went to high tea. My children were amazed that my siblings and I could so smoothly interact after such a long feud, but in face of my illness, we had all decided to put it behind us.

The next day we spent catching up. In the evening we went out for an Indian dinner. What a sense of peace and restoration I felt, spending time with my siblings! God truly does work good in seeming disasters.

We shared such a wonderful weekend for me, even with the shadow of the transplant looming over me. My siblings prayed Hindu prayers over me with me and blessed me. Nick and Zach did not participate in that and moved to the side. Out of sheer respect and reverence for my siblings, I received their blessings. I didn't want to be a stumbling block to them. Not only that, but a new glimmer of hope arose: Manju consented to talk to one of the doctors to see if there was any way she could be my donor after all. That was a step in the right direction. I thanked the Lord for it.

For my doctor's appointment on Valentine's Day, I got all dressed up in a pink jacket and skirt, and I didn't forget my wig. I felt better when I put on nice clothes and makeup. The way I looked was one thing in the journey that I could control, and it made me feel better, more normal, so I thought it was worth the effort.

Dr. Stock greeted Nick and me somberly, and we sat down across from her desk. "Anjuli, you look beautiful in that outfit." She picked up her pen. "Here's what I see for you. Are you ready?"

I nodded and took Nick's hand as she began to lay out my options, busily sketching as she spoke.

"First, we finish the chemo and hope that the cancer doesn't come back." She looked directly at me. "That hope is not likely. Second, while you're in remission, we keep looking for a bone marrow donor, hoping that we are successful before the cancer returns."

I knew that given my Indian heritage, finding a full match was also unlikely. When I'd heard the news that Manju was a full match, I felt I'd won the lottery. Now I felt like someone had stolen my ticket. As promised, Manju did meet with one of the doctors, but all I heard from that conversation was that she was unable to donate. To this day I've

CHAPTER 16: Exploring Options

never received any explanation of why, and I probably won't. Standard protocol dictates a wall between the donor and recipient that can only be breached by the consent of both parties. In fact, my doctors could not speak directly to her; only Dr. Larson, as the head of the service, was permitted to. The physician in me understood why following this procedure was necessary, but emotionally, it frustrated and angered me. Eventually I had to accept that not knowing the reason was simply one more issue I couldn't control.

Of course, the chance had always been slim—yet when I heard the news I felt as if the roof had collapsed on my head, burying me under a pile of rubble and debris I had no hope of climbing out from under. As best as I could, I worked through the disappointment and despair and prayed for God to continue to sustain me as we moved forward with my transplant.

I had to concentrate on the possibilities Dr. Stock laid out for me, not mourn those that were impossible. So while I'd keep looking for another full match, if we didn't find one quickly, we'd have to consider another option.

"Which would be?" I asked.

"Receiving a transplant from a partial match. There are two possibilities here: using umbilical cord blood from a newborn infant or using a half-matched donor." She paused as she added to her sketch and waited for my nod to indicate that I followed. "The fourth possibility is for you to donate stem cells to yourself. This would be a full match, so there would be no risk of rejection." She looked up from her paper, and I could see the compassion in her eyes. "However, while this works well with some forms of cancer, it does not for ALL."

I so appreciated how honestly Dr. Stock explained the benefits and risks of each choice before me. As she spoke, she held my hand and looked into my eyes. After discussing the matter for a while, we chose the third option. Umbilical cord blood has stem cells that can be used as the transplant. The advantage of this option was that I could receive a transplant as soon as possible, so the risk of my cancer returning while I waited was lower. And I wouldn't have to keep searching for that one brick in the city and waiting, spending precious time we would not necessarily have.

But Dr. Stock wasn't done. "Anjuli, there's a twist on all of this that I need to tell you about."

I looked at her with wide eyes, the hair on my arm standing up. I didn't want more bad news. She started a new sketch on her notepad as she explained, "We could do a new experimental procedure for your transplant."

"An experiment?"

"Yes. We will transplant both the cord blood stem cells and blood from a half-match donor. Cord blood cells take longer to engraft in the bone marrow, so it takes longer for them to begin producing blood." Her pen flew over the paper, drawing arrows and little circles to represent blood cells. "The half-match cells from an adult donor will engraft more quickly. The theory is the half-match cells will form a bridge to produce blood until the cord blood cells engraft and take over."

I was very skeptical and afraid of the idea of an experimental treatment. But knowing I didn't really have a choice, I said, "I have to choose between life and death. I will do whatever it takes to grab my life."

Nick, having read avidly on the subject, had several questions. "What have your results been with the patients who received this kind of procedure?"

Dr. Stock replied, "It is too early in the journey to say. The first review of forty-six patients will be presented at a meeting in April. Overall, we can report a positive outcome for that group." She looked directly at him. "We have modified the protocol as we have moved along and are seeing better results. I need to tell you that the University of Chicago is the only center in the country that does this procedure."

"It sounds good," said Nick, "but what are the disadvantages?"

She put down her pen. "The disadvantage is that the stem cells and the half-match donor could be rejected. To counter this rejection, we'll use powerful drugs which will further suppress Anjuli's immune system."

We discussed this new option for a while and finally agreed it was my best hope. Dr. Stock scheduled a procedure called apheresis the next week to harvest my own stem cells. The doctors wanted to have them as a backup in case something went wrong. If neither the half-match or the stem cells began producing blood cells, then I would have no source of blood. In that case, they would transplant my own cells back so that my marrow could produce blood cells. It would still produce cancer cells, but at least I would be alive to consider other options.

Once I went in for the transplant, I would be in the hospital for about a month. In the meantime, I needed to rest and build my reserves in preparation for the battle.

After all that, Nick took me out for a romantic Valentine's Day dinner at Shang Hai Terrace. Our favorite waiter, Max, served us and made a margarita for Nick exactly how he liked it. I ordered my favorite spicy eggplant. I wished I could have enjoyed it more. Halfway through the dinner, we had to leave because some of the side effects of my chemo flared up. I was feeling a little down as well, thinking of what lay ahead.

Wednesday, February 16

Today I learned that not only has my cancer gone into morphological remission, which means there are no cancer cells circulating in the blood, but even in my bone marrow, there is not much evidence of the cancer. That means there is molecular improvement and all of the medications I am taking are helpful.

I'm grateful that if I have to have cancer, it's in a time when they can do these molecular studies. Up to about ten years ago, these studies were impossible. Now they have instruments that allow them to look at my cells at a magnification of one thousand times what the naked eye can see. So I am in remission, which is the goal for this point in the treatment. We still have a long way to go to reach a cure.

I'm reminded of Psalm 86: "Hear me, Lord, and answer me, for I am poor and needy." He did answer me in my day of trouble, and delivered me from the depths of the grave, and helping and comforting me.

He has done this, as have those who have prayed so faithfully for me.

While my mind accepted the decisions we had made, my emotions spun and scattered like leaves before a driving wind. Anxious and fearful about the thought of undergoing an experimental treatment, I sought out Dr. Tobin.

She listened to me patiently, then said, "There is no way to say if this new procedure will not be a better one for you." She laid her hand on my arm. "God has picked this procedure for you for a reason we do not understand."

I thought about what she said and knew she was right.

With two weeks to go until the transplant, I concentrated on resting up as well as I could, enjoying every minute before I returned to the hospital. I watched movies, played cards, and exercised; and every chance I got, I simply enjoyed the time with my family in the apartment we had rented in Chicago. Such a blessing to be out of the hospital! I told Zach I'd never before had so much free time.

Once again, I found myself reflecting on the change that had come into my life. Despite all of its uncertainties and physical struggles, it had been a beautiful journey of connecting with the Lord. He was making me into a brand-new person. I could see the truth that He is faithful in all He does. I trusted in His holy name, whatever the outcome. And now I was hopeful that the transplant would give me a new life.

Sunday, February 20

I am so confident that the Lord is going to heal me, although I am fighting a monster, a beastly disease.

> *"Praise the LORD, my soul, and forget not all his benefits* (Psalm 103:2)."

He has summoned me, Anjuli, by name. When I pass through the waters, they will not sweep over me. When I pass through the fires, they will not burn me.

"I will heal you." That is the promise He has given me. That's all I have to go with, His word.

CHAPTER 16: Exploring Options

The transplant will not be an easy battle. Graft-versus-host disease is a real possibility, and the transplant may be rejected, but I will not fear. I will depend on the promises of God. He's already got me to Base 1, remission. Now He's going to take me to Base 2 and Base 3. He's done so much already, healing me and creating strong bonds among my family.

In late February, I asked Dr. Stock if I could delay the transplant since I was enjoying the time off from the hospital so much. She responded by saying that even a week's delay could be detrimental, and she strongly advised doing the transplant as soon as possible. She also mentioned that even though I was in remission, there was still a risk of the cancer spreading to my brain. She also advised me to get chemotherapy injected into my spine, which would be the fifth time I would have this procedure done.

My own stem cells would be collected that Monday through the apheresis procedure. I would receive shots every twelve hours for four days leading up to the apheresis so my body would produce more blood cells. One of the most difficult stages of my physical journey was about to begin.

While the apheresis was being done, the doctors will perform what they called an "access procedure." To put it simply, they will insert some tubing that will stick out so the doctors could have easy access to my body. The tubing will remain in place to be used for the transplant.

On Wednesday I am going to be admitted for at least six weeks for the transplant. The umbilical cord blood would be mixed with Zach's blood, which was a half-match. David, my other half-match, had tested positive for the Epstein-Barr virus, a result of his having had mono some years ago. This virus could be passed on to me through his blood, and as I had no immune system, it could be deadly. Zach's blood was the best match with the fewest risks attached to it.

As I prepared to leave the oasis of our Chicago apartment and return to the hospital, the future was full of unknowns.

I am hoping and praying that the donated blood cells will engraft and will take the place of my own marrow, which has been directed by my genes to make cancer cells.

There is a degree of fear and apprehension. Although I have a high pain tolerance, I still grow fearful—mostly at nighttime or early hours of the morning. Many Scriptures speak of fear and how God helps us to overcome it, telling us to "fear not" and how He watches over us. I need to be in the Scriptures at all times and leave everything to the Lord. I ask that Jesus be my banner and go ahead of me.

Together, we had committed to facing this disease head-on. Now the most critical part of that battle was about to commence.

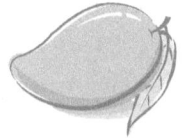

Chapter 17

The Transplant

Wednesday, February 23

I had my fifth lumbar puncture today. It seems they get more painful each time. The good news is they were able to do the apheresis through my arm veins, so they didn't have to do the access procedure today. The bad news is they couldn't harvest enough cells, so we'll have to do more apheresis next week. I'm grateful I won't have those tubes for a couple more days.

Even walking short distances takes a lot out of me. Since so much of my bone marrow has been wiped out, my body is not producing much blood. I don't have red blood cells to carry oxygen throughout my body. So I get weak and short of breath easily and can only walk on the treadmill at a tortoise's pace.

I started thinking about the gift of suffering. One of the greatest benefits I have received through this journey of cancer is something I never asked for and didn't really want. It is the gift of being able to identify with the suffering of Christ. I want to thank Jesus for the incredible physical suffering that He was able to undergo for me.

I am just hoping for complete healing here. God's blessings have come in multiple ways. Dr. Stock says I look very good and I should just whiz through this. I look outside. It's hailing, lightning, and snowing, but God has control over nature. Surely He has control over cancer.

My final eye appointment pronounced my eyes clear of inflammation, and Dr. Stock brought additional fantastic news: the umbilical cord blood I would be receiving was a slightly better match than we had expected. We had heard it matched on four of six indicators; later tests showed it matched on five.

There was still a great deal of risk. The doctors will transplant the two types of cells: the cord blood stem cells and the half-identical cells from Zach's blood. The half-identical cells are supposed to start producing cancer-free cells first. Then after about a month, the cord blood cells will take over, at least, that is the idea. There were no guarantees that either or both would happen. If the half-identical cells don't engraft, then I will be left without any cells that are able to fight infection, a dangerous situation that could last for over a month.

Another possibility is that only the half-identical cells implant, which would not be good for the long term. In that case, I would have to continue to take medicines to suppress rejection, which would involve suppressing my immune system. Since the cord blood cells were immature cells, there was a lower tendency for the body to reject them.

We waited over two hours to see Dr. Stock, but I was able to ask her many questions. Her answers relieved many of my anxieties. Nick and I agreed it was worth the wait, and we were grateful she had spent some time with us when she really had no time at all.

Saturday, February 26

I'm a little fearful about the unknown, of what will happen next week with my transplant. But I know that true love casts away all fears. I realize that my suffering makes Christ more visible to others through me. My pain has given God an opportunity to work for my own good, and I am never going to be the same again. I'm fearful, but I will continue to

CHAPTER 17: The Transplant

rejoice. I'm struggling a bit with side effects from the shots I'm getting for the apheresis. The pain medication helps, but there is still a constant achiness that will be with me for a few more days.

That evening, the family and I went to Moody Bible Church, where the elders and pastors anointed me with oil. It was something I wanted to do—a step of faith I felt I needed to take, if only to strengthen my own heart. Sometimes I felt dismayed. I had read a lot of the medical literature on stem cell transplants, and I got a little discouraged about my prognosis. But the Great Physician was holding my hand. Having people pray for me helped me remember that fact.

In the dim lighting of the sanctuary, I looked up at the cross on the wall and thought of how Jesus held in His cup the sins of the world. In my cup, I only had my leukemia. I could barely comprehend how heavy His cup was. I could not even fathom the sacrifice that He'd made. There in that quiet place, sitting in the rustic oak pews under the brass chandeliers, I found peace and calm. Colored reflections of the stained glass decorated the walls. I gazed at the words from Hebrews painted over the cross in Roman script: "Jesus Christ is the same yesterday, today, and tomorrow." I prayed that His flesh and His blood would give me the strength, perseverance, character, and hope I needed while I went for my transplant next week.

Tuesday, March 1

I went into the hospital for the apheresis yesterday. It didn't go as planned. The first thing they did was draw blood to see if I had enough stem cells. I did not. So they gave me an extra-large dose of the medicine that causes me to produce these cells.

Today I went back. Apheresis is a long procedure. Mine lasted from eight in the morning to five in the afternoon, and it didn't go completely smoothly. My veins held up, praise the Lord, so they didn't need to do the access procedure.

However, they couldn't collect enough stem cells. This meant another dose of the shot that stimulates stem cell production. It also causes a lot of pain in my bones. Tomorrow will be yet another day of apheresis.

What I'm getting is experimental. They know it works for some people, but not others, and they have no idea why. So in case neither the half-match or the cord blood cells engraft, they need my own cells to get my marrow (and blood production) functioning again. I can only trust in God's sovereign hand.

Two long days of apheresis took their toll. I was discouraged, thinking that since the apheresis wasn't going well, the upcoming larger battle of the transplant might also go badly. I repeated verses from the Bible to push away the fear. On Thursday the access procedure was performed, but my blood wasn't clotting. The apheresis had taken all of my platelets, and without platelets, no clotting. The doctors finally got the bleeding to stop, but I knew it could start again.

They weren't able to stop the pain. Those tubes made me feel like I had something boring into my body that did not belong there. They reminded me of cancer every time I was aware of their presence, even when I shifted positions in my sleep. I had the constant sensation of an irritant from which I longed to escape.

Adding to my worries, I had a sense that the conflict in the family was getting worse, not better. I knew Nick had come down hard on David for something and that David and Zach were quarrelling. They all tried to keep the details from me. But I'm a mother, and I worry anyway. This emotional tension was simply one more burden to bear when I didn't feel I could bear much more. I did all I could to stay positive, but some days, it just wasn't possible.

That Friday was a bit better, with no more bleeding. The intense chemotherapy that was designed to knock out all of my bone marrow was started. I began to feel the debilitating side effects, the dizziness, nausea and vomiting, diarrhea.

Sunday, March 6

Today was better. The medicines they gave me for the side effects of the chemo are helping, but they have side effects of their own. At least I can still read my Bible, for that gives me strength and hope.

CHAPTER 17: The Transplant

Zach came to see me, showing off his newly shaved head, proclaiming, "Bald is beautiful." This is the second time in this long journey that he's shaved off his hair in solidarity with me. He says whether this is a long journey, or as it feels like, a horrible nightmare that will not end, it's a marathon, and we are in it together.

I read Psalm 139 again, and the chapter ministers so to my spirit. I have decided that I am going to use the time given to me well. Every minute of this journey I am going to learn more and more about Jesus and get into a deeper relationship with Him, and I am going to thank Him for the things I have never before experienced. I strive to enjoy the sufferings because even though my body is wasting away, internally it is being rejuvenated by the Spirit of Christ as I look forward to the prize that is laid up for me in heaven.

Monday I was given some blood, which helped alleviate my fatigue. They would continue to give me lots of blood since I would have so little of my own. My bone marrow was being destroyed to make way for the transplanted cells, so my body had no way to make blood cells. Until the transplanted cells engrafted and began producing blood cells, I would have no protection against infection. Zach said I would be like a castle with no walls, a prime target for invaders. So I was moved to an isolation room with a special air vent system that sucked out airborne bacteria. Everyone who came in had to wash his hands and wear gloves, masks, and gowns. I wore a mask most of time.

I felt like I was in an aseptic prison, a prison constructed for my own good, but a prison nonetheless. Even Nick could not touch me during this time. While with my mind I understood the scientific reasons for this, I felt abandoned and alone. Intellectually, I was prepared. I didn't realize how my emotions would trump what my mind knew to be facts. Even with all of our precautions, it would only take one invading microbe to give me a nasty infection that could end my life. I called upon God's protection against infection and put my trust in Him. Our Heavenly Father is sovereign, even over microbes.

Various side effects of my medications, including a rash, nausea, and vomiting were fading away thanks to other medications. The diarrhea, however, continued. One of the drugs being used was mustard gas, which burns the entire digestive system from mouth to anus. I had to chew ice or have something cold in my mouth for six hours continuously. The ice prevented ulcers from forming in my mouth. I was so happy when someone thought to bring me a popsicle as a change from all of the ice!

By Wednesday I only had a little nausea, no vomiting or diarrhea. The hardest part of the day was keeping something cold in my mouth for six hours. As annoying as that was, I was grateful there was nothing worse going on.

Someone shared with me a list of ten reasons not to waste my cancer. They inspired me to focus on Christ and not simply on what I wanted. Through my website and phone calls, I was hearing from friends and relatives from whom I hadn't heard in years. Thinking of these things helped me to keep from despair when I was feeling my worst.

Thursday night, I had a bad reaction to one of my medications, with swelling, rash, and redness all over my body. I was administered more medicine. By the afternoon I was doing much better, even though I was receiving two medicines continuously, then a third through another access point. Since I was on so many drugs, the doctor didn't know which one was causing the reaction, but they thought it was one that would be discontinued soon. I could only hope so. The following day I would get the transplant itself, and I knew they might use all five access points in my chest.

I chose not to focus on those details. Instead, I was able to enjoy some time with my family, looking at David's wedding pictures with Luke, watching a *Golden Girls* rerun with Alicia. Tomorrow was the big day.

I was as ready as I would ever be.

Saturday, March 12

I received my bone marrow transplant yesterday. I was heavily medicated to prevent any rejection. A side effect of that medication is drowsiness, so I slept most of the day.

CHAPTER 17: The Transplant

Today was an arduous day, with lots of diarrhea, which they tell me could last up to a week. Most of the day I have felt lousy—real lousy. I could not even concentrate to read the Word of God.

But somehow a reservoir of strength and power came to mind: Romans 8. If we don't know how to pray, it doesn't matter. He does our praying for us, making prayers out of our groans. For many years, I have made a habit out of Bible study and prayer. But recently, because of the chemo-induced fatigue, my Bible simply doesn't get much attention. My thoughts are consumed with merely breathing and fighting nausea or coping with any one of the different physical symptoms I feel.

I try to push myself a little harder, to see if I can navigate this treatment with greater success. But each day it gets a little tougher. Somewhere in the middle of this, grace has entered in. I remember that God did not change when I was diagnosed with cancer. I am grateful that my life with God does not depend on my performance. In my weakness and disability, His Spirit wages war on my behalf. I pray that He will take away the diarrhea, the dehydration, the depression.

Sunday, March 13

I'm still having the diarrhea and having trouble eating. I know I need to eat, but the nausea takes away any desire. Having no red cells gives me fatigue I never imagined, fatigue that leaves me unable to get out of bed or even think about trying to stand. The transfusions help, but they are not enough.

I need prayers so badly. I'm very depressed and don't know why. So many symptoms—headache, diarrhea, nausea, body aches—are becoming unbearable for me. How will I ever be able to go on? I just can't take any more of this.

Monday, March 14

Today was a little better. The diarrhea has just about gone away. My white count is next to nothing, which is what we expected.

I am dependent on God totally. In Ephesians, Paul says that God can do more than we can ask or imagine. I feel so physically, emotionally, and spiritually beaten—partly because of the medicines and staying in the hospital. The headaches and body aches are severe, and the pain medicines make me so groggy that I can't read the Scriptures. I look at the blog and see the notes and prayers people have left there. That makes me feel better and helps me to rely on Christ.

I have been so blessed by the presence of my family. Along with Nick, the boys, and Alicia, and my sister-in-law, Indira, has been here, as has my younger sister. Mridul took a week off of work to stay here with me. She and Indira have tirelessly fed me ice, which soothes my burnt-out digestive tract, and have cared for me in countless ways. What I would do without their tender assistance I don't know.

Tuesday, March 15

On Tuesday, Alicia and David helped me open my cards. It's so encouraging to receive them, to know people are thinking of me and praying for me. I was also able to walk down the hall twice, accompanied by my faithful IV stand. Being able to walk is a big accomplishment.

I'm still so weak and frail with my white count at zero. I don't feel too good today, and I developed a fever. That's a big problem, as fever could be a sign of some kind of infection.

Wednesday, March 16

The doctors established that I have a generalized blood infection due to E. coli from my belly, which for someone in my condition is a medical emergency. More drugs for me to take, this time antibiotics.

Thursday, March 17

Some improvement. The fever is gone; the antibiotics continue. I can walk up and down the hallways a little more, and I'm eating more. White count is still zero.

CHAPTER 17: The Transplant

Friday, March 18

God is touching me every day, and I feel so much better from how I felt on Sunday. Things haven't changed much—still no platelets, my immune system is washed out. The pain is much better. I have renewed faith and comfort in our Lord Jesus Christ.

I feel that every day is a new day in Jesus. I'm hoping in the next seven days Zach's blood cells will graft in me, that they will begin producing blood cells, which will bring me energy, protection, and strength.

Saturday, March 19

Yesterday I developed another fever. They did tests to see if it was the same infection as before. It wasn't as bad as the first. I'm also having a lot of stomach pain. While they give me painkillers, I just have to ride it out as best I can.

Today brought relief from the fever and the diarrhea. I'm having a lot of pain in my chest, stomach and belly, which is a side effect of one of my medicines. This pain is *mucositis*, which is inflammation of the mucosa of my digestive tract. I can't eat much because whatever I swallow irritates the mucosa, causing a lot of pain and discomfort.

I am feeling good enough to look at some magazines, like a *People* magazine covering the Oscars. Such fun to look at the dresses the famous women wore!

Tuesday, March 22

Thanks to some medicine that seems to be helping with the mucositis, I've been able to nibble a bit on some food the past two days. Fever and diarrhea seem to be gone.

This waiting process is a marathon that has no set finish line. I'm simply waiting for the graft to happen. There's nothing I can do to speed it up. I pray fervently every day that my graft will show up. Today is the ninth day. It can happen as early as day seven. So far it hasn't. We still wait.

When David filmed me for my blog, I asked my listeners if they were feeling sick or miserable or if the world seemed drab and dreary. So I shared with them a little thought to help them feel more cheery. "Death is just a stepping stone to a life we have never known."

Wednesday, March 23

Yesterday we saw some evidence of Zach's cells grafting into my bone marrow. It's just really slow, slower than a stalactite forming. My total blood count is only twelve. This is about one one-thousandth of a normal count. I praise God, because no matter how slow, it's in the right direction. I am pleased, delighted, enthusiastic, thankful, blessed, and above all, grateful to God. My pains are much improved because my medications have been changed.

I watch every morning for my cell count. I wake up at 6:30 and watch the clock until eight, when I get the results. I have become rather obsessed with my blood counts. I try to rely not on myself, but on the work of the Holy Spirit in me, which has brought me up to this point.

Thursday, March 24

Today we got the great news: I have engrafted! Zach's cells are now producing healthy blood cells. I feel great! No more cancer cells—just healthy ones growing. It is a process that will take a while. A lot of toxic materials have gone into my system, but God is glorious and victorious. So far I have come through. Everything that I have gone through only brings glory to Him.

While the chemo-induced nausea and fatigue were at their worst, my Bible sat and collected dust on the bedside table. My thoughts were consumed with my illness. I had convinced myself that if I tried just a little harder or pushed myself a little more, I could navigate this journey more confidently. Now I knew it was God Who worked in me.

David and I celebrated the successful graft with a big meal of Indian food; then I succumbed to a food coma and slept. It was the first of

CHAPTER 17: The Transplant

many big meals: for the next several days, I found myself eating like a horse. The pain I'd experienced swallowing was gone, so it was no longer so difficult to eat. That was good, since I would need a lot of energy to produce new blood cells! Bone marrow typically weighs about six pounds, and it produces 220,000,000,000 red blood cells each day. That number doesn't include the white blood cells it also produces.

My counts climbed daily. But even with this good news, I was feeling a bit down. The process had been long, and it had taken its toll on me. Facing life and death. Going through months of controlled amounts of poison infused into my body. Being continuously intruded upon, violated with needles and examinations. Not having a moment's peace. Only God knew fully what I had endured.

Soon I would be discharged, but the journey was still far from over. I would have to come back for monitoring. The doctors would be looking for two major things. The first was any sign of graft-versus-host disease. Essentially, this would be my body (the host) rejecting the graft, considering it to be a danger to me like a bacteria or virus. I was on large doses of antirejection medications, but this was a still a risk. The second was signs that the umbilical cord blood cells had engrafted. The theory was that once the cord blood cells engrafted, the half-match cells would phase out. Over the next few months, we would see how well this experimental treatment was working for me.

But I was so tired. As a matter of fact, we were all tired, and it showed. There was more strife among us, which didn't help anyone.

I clung to God's Word, to His promise that His loving-kindness endures forever. Time and again, I had seen it revealed to me. I did not know one day to the next what would happen. But I knew that whether I was on this side or the other of the curtain, I would be able to thank Him. I knew that nothing but good would come out of this. Yes, there would be bumps in the way. But there was still hope in our Savior, the Lord Jesus Christ. There was *good* in store for me. I did all I could to stand on that truth.

Sometimes I grew despondent. I hoped the melancholy would all be gone one day, as it was a trial in itself. My Zach told me that when

I felt that way, I should try to pray. Following his advice helped me tremendously.

By Monday, I was feeling somewhat better, and I would even get a chance to exercise later on. David tried to have me show a picture to the camera as he was filming for my blog. I told him, "I cannot function at the rate you want me to respond." We laughed at that. That kind of response showed me my energy was coming back. I simply had to let go of being able to do all I used to do and as quickly. David asked me how my mood was today. "On that blog, I'm going to tell you it's great," I answered.

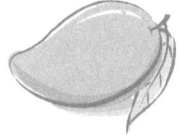

Chapter 18
Beginning to Hope

March 29 was a great day for me: I was discharged from the hospital after one month from the transplant. My immune system had been completely replaced by Zach's blood and the cord blood. They were starting to work, though not as quickly as we wanted them to.

I also received another surprise. When Dr. Stock handed me the cytogenetic report, which was the report of test results that showed the cord blood was engrafting, I noticed that the engraftment analysis stated that my new cells bore the XY chromosome instead of the XX that females had. I was aghast. I imagined that this transplant was turning me into a man.

"Dr. Stock," I said, "Am I going to get a beard?"

She laughed. "No, Anjuli, the XY chromosome is a result of your grafted cells which were obtained from the blood of a male infant's umbilical cord. Whatever the source of the grafted cells the genotype may change, but the phenotype will stay the same."

In other words, because the cells now producing blood in my body are from a male, these blood cells will carry the XY chromosome. However, I will still be a woman and still look like a woman!

The news was shocking as I was not prepared to learn from a cytogenetic report that my chromosomes were now XY. No one had told me that I was receiving blood from a male infant's cord, and even if that fact had been mentioned, I was unaware of this possible outcome. Of course, that information wouldn't have changed anything. My options were to take the transplant from the cord blood or risk death. That the chromosomes in my blood would change from female to male was a small price to pay for a chance at life.

After I left the hospital, Nick and I checked into a hotel. I didn't have much appetite and was still weak. The home-cooked meals we had delivered looked tasty, but after a few bites, I was done.

I thanked God when I remembered those who faithfully prayed for me. Their blog comments and e-mails and cards kept me going through the day, letting me know the family of Christ works together, weeps together, and rejoices together. It was a beautiful feeling—this community we had.

Throughout the day as a rule, I stayed in bed. I would get up and walk around a little bit, then go back to bed, mostly because of the weakness of my body. I would be going back to the hospital for blood transfusions since I had almost no blood left. I prayed that as my new bone marrow made more blood cells, more energy would come into my body and that all of the cancer cells would finally be eliminated.

Thoughts of my family were a welcome distraction. I prayed for Luke as he was making decisions about which college to go to. He had changed his plans somewhat based on my cancer, and the whole process had been nerve-racking for him.

Two days after my discharge, I felt dejected. I had hoped to bounce back to a place much better than where I was, and although my doctors continued to tell me I was doing very well, I wanted to be feeling better *now*.

At least I was able to enjoy watching Moody Bible Institute's Sunday service over the Internet. The sermon that Sunday was on the Good Samaritan, and the pastor talked about God's mercy. His address was enriching to my soul; I was feeling God's mercy step-by-step every day of my life.

The cord blood graft was starting to work, and although at times I felt like I'd been trampled down, I could cheer up when I said, "Satan,

CHAPTER 18: Beginning to Hope

I spit on you. I want you to get behind me." I could put a smile on my face and fill my mind with Scriptures. *The Lord truly is my Rock and my Redeemer,* I would remind myself. *I do have a deadly enemy, but it is God's battle, and I have claimed this victory. Everything is changing inside me, a new life that has come from the Lord.*

Slowly, I improved physically and mentally. I was still weak, and I continued to fight nausea and vomiting. My medications schedule had me taking nearly forty pills every day. The infusions of blood products helped with the weariness, but some of the medicines I was given to prevent reactions made me as sleepy as if I had been awake for days.

The first week home ended on a positive note. I had more energy and felt stronger, and Luke had been accepted into the six-year medical school program in Kansas City. After living so long day by day, I was beginning to see glimmers of a future.

Wednesday, April 12

Our thirty-third wedding anniversary was April 6, so Nick and I went out to dinner. We had to come home early because I wasn't feeling well. Every day I feel a little bit better. Boy, was it hard at the beginning. The pain of cancer is physically immeasurable. I never could have borne it without the help of Jesus Christ.

I keep thinking of Psalm 139, how God wove me together in my mother's womb, how He knew the direction my life would take and even about my cancer. This understanding helps me keep my focus on the Lord because I believe He has given me a few more years.

My spirits go up and down. The side effects of the medications add up. Some create a metallic taste in my mouth; others cause nausea, a loss of appetite, or an upset stomach. I sleep two hours in order to have fifteen minutes of energy. A lot has changed for this woman who used to fly halfway around the world and back without skipping a beat. Sometimes the weakness and side effects are too much. I cry a lot.

I know God allowed ALL to come upon me and that He will not allow Satan to win. I know it is His power that will help me to be healed.

I've been very mopey, feeling sorry for myself with all my aches and pains, the nausea, diarrhea, headaches. These physical symptoms created a wall between me and the Almighty, as if I was in a dark dungeon, chained up behind bars. Then I read in Philippians that Paul wanted to learn to be content in all circumstances. So I pray to be like Paul, and when I do get my attention off of my dark moods or physical pain, it's like a ray of sunshine has penetrated into my jail cell. I simply need to focus on Him. I will be His follower, and He will be my leader, my healer.

In these four months, I have not had one good night's sleep. But what rest I get, I rest in the shadow of the Almighty and gaze upon the beauty of the Lord.

Yesterday my friend Nancy came to see me for the first time. As my white count has risen, my doctor allows me to have visitors. Being able to speak with people on the phone has helped, but seeing a dear friend in person lifts up my heart. I rejoice in the hope I have that one day I will see Jesus face-to-face.

Emotionally I am a yo-yo, which happens to many cancer patients. I go between feeling like I'm trapped in a cage and feeling set free. I pray for greater emotional stability.

Today was a long day at the hospital, getting blood infused into my body. Tomorrow I go back for more, including a bone marrow biopsy.

Spring arrived. As time passed after my transplant, the days started to merge together. I no longer thought just hour by hour, day by day, but could see my way to think in terms of weeks and months. No longer did I wake up wondering if this would be my last day.

In mid-April, Dr. Stock permitted me to return home to Bloomington for four or five days. I was slowly gaining strength, and I loved seeing familiar faces and enjoyed being back in my home. I could see my dog, Sergio, walk around my house, and I could have a little more space. I didn't take a moment for granted. Life would never be the same again. I rested in the thought that I might have cancer with a small "c," but I also had the big "C"—Christ. He would overcome the small "c."

I enjoyed seeing the tulips come up, watching the ducks on the lake, and even seeing two white swans. I kept the window open morning

CHAPTER 18: Beginning to Hope

and night and listened to the birds' chirping. It all brought to mind the goodness of God and the control He had over nature, like the rising and the setting of the sun. Again I thought of Psalm 103:2-3, where it says, "Praise the LORD, my soul, and forget not all his benefits, who forgives all your sins and heals all your diseases."

While I basked in the warmth of the spring and the familiarity of home, I received a report saying that morphologically, no cancer cells were present in my bone marrow. The graft was taking place in its own time. God was healing my diseases and redeeming my life; He was crowning me with love and compassion. I praised the Lord for where He had brought me since the tenth of December. Mine had been a long and painful journey, often two steps forward and one step back. I had learned to cry out to Him in a way I had never before known. He snatched me from the jaws of death and rejuvenated me so I could answer His calling on my life on this earth.

I thought of Abraham: when his body was as good as dead, he did not waver but trusted God's promise. That was exactly how I felt: that my body was as good as dead. Sometimes I became self-centered and quit focusing on God. That's when I would get depressed and start crying. As Easter approached, I prayed that I would have the strength to go to church and worship. In the meantime, I would stand firm and wait on the Lord.

We went back to Chicago for a few days for some doctor's appointments and follow-up tests. The initial results of the biopsy show no cancer under the microscope, and my bone marrow was doing well. Over the next few weeks, we would find out which of the transplanted cells were producing blood cells and if any cancer was detected at the level of the DNA. This was a measure one million times more precise than the analysis done under the microscope.

I wasn't able to attend Easter services in spite of my prayers, but I watched Moody's service on television. It was wonderful to watch the choir, the worship. By the grace of God and the prayers of the saints, I was feeling better. I was fighting a little skin infection, and I prayed for its quick healing.

The day after Easter, I had another appointment with Dr. Stock. She entered the room wearing her white coat and a broad, beaming smile. "Your DNA results are back. None of the cells in your body are your original cancer cells, and basically, you are considered cancer free."

"This is a miracle!" I screamed, and we hugged one another. Over her shoulder I saw Nick stand to his feet and applaud, saying, "Anjuli, you made it!"

When we calmed down, we all sat, and Dr. Stock continued, sketching as always. "The blood cells you are producing are a mixture, with some from the cord blood graft and some from the half-matched cells, which was what we expected at this point. Your white count, platelets count, and hemoglobin are all doing very well."

"I am still feeling weak, and I have a lot of muscle pains and achiness."

"Around the seventy-fifth day of your graft, these symptoms should all disappear. You will grow stronger, and you should see a great change on the hundredth day of the transplant."

"I can hardly wait for that hundredth day!" Once I made it that far, I would really be able to believe that I could survive this cancer and start a new life.

My days were spent recuperating. One result of my transplant was that I had lost all of the immunity I ever had, so even though I had an occasional visitor, I had to be very careful not to be around people. My white count was still low but growing slowly. My platelet counts were also up, so I no longer needed transfusions of platelets and blood. I was weak and unstable like an infant when I walked.

Soon Zach would graduate from medical school. I so much wanted to be able to attend the ceremony, at least parts of it. There would be overcrowding, people sitting close together—not an atmosphere that would be congenial for me. The decision would be made hour by hour, depending on my strength.

There were high points in all of this. My children made a video tribute for me for Mother's Day. I also had another vision of the Lord.

I'm not certain exactly when it was, but it came soon after I returned to Bloomington. I was not sleeping well at the time. Often, if I couldn't sleep, I would get on my knees and start praying. This particular night I had just gotten up from my prayer time, lain down on the bed, and fell into a deep slumber. An angel of the Lord clad in white came. This woman with a bright face looked at me with firm eyes and said, "I will give you one more chance." Suddenly there was a bright light, and I woke up. I jumped up out of my bed, shouting, trying to catch the angel.

I woke up Nick, who was sleeping on the couch. "Nick, I just saw an angel!"

He looked at me through half-opened eyes and said, "Go back to bed." I understood he thought I was hallucinating. That's okay; I know what I saw.

I've thought much about what the angel said. For what was God giving me one more chance? Something I needed to do? Something He wanted to do in me?

May 10 marked five months from my diagnosis. I had come a long way. My chemotherapy was done; my transplant had engrafted. On the molecular level, I was almost completely free of cancer. On the other hand, my CMV level—cytomegalovirus, which can cause complications in the eyes and liver—was rising. This finding was not surprising, as I had been exposed to CMV earlier in life. I would be starting a new medication for that condition, and I prayed it would be effective. Thankfully, I was allowed to go back to Bloomington for nine days of recuperation.

A week later, I went back to my office for the first time. To get it ready for me, my staff sanitized my private office, and I went in the back door to avoid exposure to the patients. I was trying to start doing small things that would make me feel useful again.

As June drew near, I realized anew how close God had come to me in rescuing me from this cancer. I praised Him when my latest peripheral blood test for DNA, which is the molecular diagnosis for cancer cells, said that the replicates for my gene were still positive but below the level of calibration, so they were not detectably measurable. Our goal was that they would become completely negative.

By early June, I noticed a definite growth of the hair on my head. Instead of being completely bald, I now sported a very short crew cut.

There were other changes in our lives. June 6 marked the day Zach left for Baltimore to start his residency at Johns Hopkins. This was unknown territory for both him and us, but I felt confident that this was where God had called him. After his training, his utmost desire was to set up a medical center for poor and destitute people who did not have access to health care, so that he could serve them with compassion and the heart of Christ. He was fulfilling my heart's desire to serve the poor. I thought back to the destitute people I had treated as a medical student in India and felt a sense of joy that my Zach wanted to dedicate his life to easing their pain.

The first verse I ever read in the Bible was Acts 2:38–9: "Repent and be baptized, every one of you, in the name of Jesus Christ for the forgiveness of your sins. And you will receive the gift of the Holy Spirit. The promise is for you and your children and for all who are far off—for all whom the Lord our God will call." I believed, as I said goodbye to my son, that today this commission from Acts 2 was being fulfilled in Zach. He was being called to go afar to spread the word of Jesus Christ, and I committed him into God's hands—just as I was trusting God for my life, whatever blessings or trials would yet come my way.

Chapter 19
Relapse

On July 27, I went to the hospital to have blood drawn as usual. My consultation with Dr. Stock did not go as I had expected.

After a long wait, Dr. Stock came to the examination room. She pulled up the test results on the screen, and we saw that my blood counts had doubled in one week.

"Don't worry, Anjuli. I have seen this phenomenon at times with patients who had the cord stem cell transplant."

As much as I wanted to believe her, I couldn't. "No, Dr. Stock," I said. "I bet you I have blasts in my blood. I'd like for you to go to the hematopathologist and look at the smear."

Right away, accompanied by her residents, she marched down to the lab. I waited patiently, but anxiously, in the sterile exam room, focusing my mind on Psalm 91. Nick spent the time rubbing my shoulders, offering what comfort he could through his touch. He knew what was coming.

Thirty minutes later Dr. Stock returned. Those thirty minutes seemed like thirty days.

She entered the room, her head hanging down to her chest. "I am so upset," she said. "I never expected this." She took a deep breath. "Your peripheral smear is full of blasts."

It took a minute for the news to sink in. My cancer had returned.

"Are you going to do a bone marrow biopsy?" I asked.

"Yes. Go to the procedure room; we'll do it immediately."

I had multiple questions. I did not know if I would have to go through another transplant or if my death sentence was about to be handed down. I walked to the procedure room and lay down on the bed. One of Dr. Stock's colleagues, Dr. Van Besien, came by, and with compassion filling his eyes, said, "Anjuli, take heart. It will be okay. Wendy is very upset right now. She'll be here as soon as possible."

Dr. Stock came into the room fifteen minutes later. She held my hand and wept with me. "This is the nature of the disease, Anjuli," she said. After she did the procedure, she told me, "I'm going to start you on a new medicine that I hope will help. If it does, you won't have to go through another round of chemo. We'll do another bone marrow in six weeks to find out."

All the way home, I struggled to keep myself centered. *I need to rest in the Lord. Every circumstance that comes to me has passed through Christ and comes to me with a great purpose for me. I hope that my testimony of God's faithfulness can help others through the dark times in their lives. So I thank God for this one more test. His will be done.*

After a few days, Nick took a blood sample to our local hospital for analysis. The numbers had gone down, and the blasts had decreased. Dr. Stock was delighted. She wanted me to continue with a new medication called Spyrcell, which is a tyrosine kinase inhibitor that redirects the gene. The cancer cells were .00003 in my blood, so one clone had grown up and started multiplying, causing my relapse.

I continued the Sprycell as requested, but I also sought healing in another way: I prayed that the relapse would disappear. Psalm 40:4a tells us, "Blessed is the one who trusts in the Lord." There is power in prayer, and I had learned that lesson well. The Spirit intercedes for me when I don't know what to say and my head is a total blank. Zach came from Baltimore, David called me, and I felt again the blessing of having my family surrounding me.

CHAPTER 19: Relapse

Another week passed. I received the good news that my blood count was back to normal. We didn't know what the bone marrow looked like, but that would be tested in two weeks.

The Lord has given me some insights in this struggle, mostly about the power of prayer. I have for the past several weeks identified myself with the Lord Jesus Christ. I would get huffed off at God, but that was when I wasn't identified with Christ. Of course, I was hoping that my cancer would never reoccur. But it did. And that's okay. Because I am still in the will of the Father, and He is in control. I'm so grateful for that, and I want for the time I have left on this earth to do His will and to be glorifying to Him. If He wants me to live and to fulfill a purpose, I am available. I will do my best to fulfill that purpose.

I am trying so hard to trust God and not myself. This is one of the hardest challenges I am facing.

On August 9, I was readmitted to the hospital. My relapse had been taken care of with the kinase inhibitors. Morphologically and hematologically, my cancer disappeared again. But I had a high-grade fever considered to be life threatening, so I was brought back to find out what was causing it. I thought I'd be in the hospital for three or four days. It was two weeks before I was released. All kinds of tests were done for infection, looking for the cause of my fever. The search turned up nothing. Praise the Lord, there was no infection—none in the lung, blood, or urine. Finally the doctors discovered that the Spyrcell was causing the fever. So I was able to return home and rest.

At this time, a revelation came to me. There is a connection between prayer and trusting God. Many times we pray with tears and with the deepest feelings of our hearts. After the prayer is done, we don't fully trust God or we fail to acknowledge that He has us in the palm of His hand, that He never slumbers. He's awake all of the time, taking care of us.

I was trying to feel this assurance myself, by studying the Psalms, reading the Bible, and being in the Word at all times. But the burden was not lifted from my heart. Finally I realized that I had to let the Holy Spirit do this work in me. By myself, I could do nothing. Through Him, everything is possible. What will happen tomorrow, I do not know. I will spend my time being with Him. Because of these eight months, I had a deeper relationship with Him. I wondered if that was the reason He wanted me to be around longer—to keep developing that relationship. I also had a deeper relationship with my husband and my children that could not be replaced by anything.

As we prepared to go for our next doctor's appointment, I prayed that my hope and faith and courage would stay in the right place—fixed on the Lord.

In late August 2011, we returned to the University of Chicago, and Dr. Stock started me on monthly chemo. She planned to monitor me closely to observe the status of the cancer. It seemed that not all of my bone marrow cells had been eradicated, and some of them had started producing blood—the blood that bore cancer cells. They hoped to detect the cancer cells when they were only in the bone marrow and hadn't spread to my bloodstream.

To test my blood on the molecular level, a reverse copy of my DNA would have to be made and that copy expanded up to 27,600 times. Several times when this test had been done, the cancer was undetectable. Yet somehow, some of my cancer-producing cells had survived. I clung to Scripture, trying to stay focused and positive. The good news was that over 90 percent of my blood was being produced by the umbilical cord blood transplant, which meant the graft was fully functioning.

Scripture I had memorized came to mind, such as 1 Thessalonians 5:16–18: "I will rejoice always, pray without ceasing, and give thanks in all circumstances, for this is God's will in Christ Jesus for you."

I do not know what the Lord has for me. But I have decided to trust Him, obey Him, rejoice in Him, praise Him, worship Him, and thank Him. Never does the thought cross my mind, *Why has the cancer appeared in my body? Why am I taking all these medications?*

So many good things have come out of it. I look so slender. At fifty-seven, what woman would not want to look like me? I'm now size 4 or 6; I used to be a size 12. Not that I am saying cancer is the best way to lose weight, but it helps to find a little humor in everything. My hair has grown back. I like the snazzy salt-and-pepper look.

CHAPTER 19: Relapse

I'm sleeping well, and I have a lot of time to be in the Word and fellowship with God's people. Every day is like sweet honey that comes from the Lord to me. I'm so grateful for my family, my sweet sister-in-law, Indira, who cooks for me, and my kids who call and Skype.

Relapse or not, it's okay, because I'm in the will of the Father. I thank God for what He has revealed to me through this journey of cancer, and I feel that I'm only seeing the tip of the iceberg.

I seek His beauty, mercy, love and compassion, assurance and promises, friendship and fatherhood. I cannot get enough of it. It is such a joy to be in His Word, to be praying. He has assured me that there will be healing. He is the God Who heals. He is the Chief of Staff, the Great Physician.

September rolled around, another month in a journey that had begun ten months earlier. Before my cancer, it was much easier for me to fill my life with activity, with serving God. However, waiting, standing still, trusting Him fully, depending on Him to work—these were harder for me. He had taken control of every situation in my life: my treatment, my health, my family, my practice, my patients, my finances, my brothers and sisters. And I saw packages of small miracles every day.

I can say from my experience with cancer that God is worthy to be trusted. His plan is the greatest plan for us. All of us should invest in eternity. Our life on this earth is so short, but eternity is forever. We need to get familiar with that eternity. I don't know how much longer I have in this life, but I can look forward to spending eternity with the Almighty Father.

I'm only human—like anyone else. But the Lord has given me such joy in my life through the cancer. If I had not gotten cancer on December 10, I would have missed out on so much—knowing and loving God more intimately, experiencing the dancing that comes from knowing who we are in Christ Jesus.

I have to be honest: for most of us, just the sound of the word *cancer* fills our hearts with fear and dread. Indeed, cancer is a terrifying diagnosis. So many friends I know didn't deserve to die of cancer. Cancer does take away loved ones from us far too soon. But cancer cannot destroy my faith or erase my love for the Lord.

During all of this time, I had also been able to respond to comments on my blog, to cards, and to phone calls. I've even been in communication with people I'd never met who posted encouraging comments.

At this stage in my journey, nothing was certain. The future still depended on so many things. I knew I had two choices. I could sit and cry, wallowing in fear. Or I could face the cancer with courage. Ten years before, I had started praying with my prayer partner, "God, make us women of courage." God had surely answered those prayers.

On my blog, I said,

I have gone through so much physical pain, medications, fevers, blood draws, lines, scopes, but when I think about the nails into Jesus' wrists, and how He was hung on the cross, all of the pain I feel tends to fade away.

I keep finding new areas of my life where I need to rely on God. As a physician and a strong woman, I relied on myself. Not anymore. His grace is sufficient for me. The more vulnerable I am, the more I submit and surrender to Him, the more I know that He watches over me.

We may all fear death, but death is simply the beginning of the new life in the New Jerusalem. We are all conquerors in Christ Jesus, and we will all see victory over death.

September started miserably, with the side effects of chemotherapy. My mouth filled with ulcers and grew inflamed; it was difficult to swallow or talk because of the burning sensation, as if I had swallowed acid. On top of that, I suffered from severe stomach pain. I still wanted to praise God, saying, "Though you have made me see troubles, many and bitter, you will restore my life again (Psalm 71:20a)." I knew that I would one day be released from all of these physical trials and tribulations, but I still felt so desolate. I was vulnerable and in pain, and I could only trust in God.

Finally, on September 7, I was admitted to the hospital. My discomfort and pain had grown to the point where I needed to be hospitalized, both for better pain control and for some testing to discover the cause of so much pain.

Test after test was performed to determine what was causing my severe bellyache. Praise God, all of the tests were normal. It seemed

CHAPTER 19: Relapse

that one of the tyrosine kinase inhibitors, Nilotinib, was causing the pain. The following day, the doctor planned to switch the drug back to Sprycell. Despite the short-term relief, I knew we weren't in the clear yet. I'd had previous problems with Sprycell—this drug had caused a life-threatening fever. I prayed that I could better tolerate the medicine this time around because, quite simply, my life depended upon it.

I do not know why I have had so many stumbling blocks. Yet the Lord always assures me that He will rescue me because He loves me. I do not know why, but again and again Psalm 27:13 comes to me: "I remain confident of this: I will see the goodness of the LORD in the land of the living."

I think that after all of these obstructions I've overcome in these first nine months, there will be a silver lining. I have seen that the Enemy has attacked me, breathing out violence. But he will not be the victor. God will intervene and provide the right medication for me.

I've seen one silver lining already. Zach was able to come for the weekend, and we talked about many things, spiritual and emotional. It was wonderful. He told me to take heart and be strong. That's what I'm going to be. Courageous in the Lord, whether or not He heals me.

A day later, the bellyache was better. Never in my life had I experienced such pain for an entire week! My bowels were also cleared, bringing much relief. While I felt better in that regard, I was now running a fever, and once again, we did not know the cause of it. Though all I wanted was to go home, I would be staying in the hospital for a while yet.

A day later, my condition had worsened, with my fever becoming high grade. They thought it was a virus, and I started receiving chemo to kill it. My abdominal pain improved and I could eat, but the virus made me so weak I could not even lift up my head. I had to use a commode next to my bed. I was also being treated with antibiotics—in case it was a bacterial infection. At least I had been able to tolerate the Sprycell this time around—so far.

Sometimes I wondered why this had come on to me, but then John 9 reminded me. The disciples asked Jesus why a man was blind: was it because he had sinned or his parents had sinned? Jesus replied that the man was blind so that God's power would be revealed. I held on to that explanation: I was going through this so that His power would be shown in me. I was so weak I could barely video blog, speaking through the tears. I hoped the next day would be better.

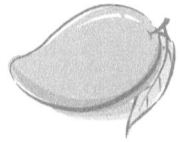

Chapter 20
The Journey Onward

What a difference a week makes! Six days after I lay in the hospital, sobbing through my pain, I was home in Bloomington with the energy to get all dressed up, stand on the deck, and have Zach film a blog post. It was such a pleasure to have him around the house. Family means so much, especially when one member has cancer. Zach's visit was an added tool God used in my healing.

On this particular day, the reality of that really hit me. My emotions went up and down like an out-of-control elevator. Sometimes I was crying, sometimes elated. I decided to keep my heart calm because the Lord had taken over this battle. Exodus 14:14 came to mind: "The LORD will fight for you, you need only to be still." In the first few months of my cancer, I prayed for His help. I no longer prayed that way. When I was praying for His help, a component of me wanted to do things in my own strength. I wanted to do this *with* Him. Now I only wanted to rely on God, to stand firm and to let God fight my battles.

I did not know why this Scripture had come to me now and not six months before. But God's timing was perfect. All I could do was stand firm and let Him do the fighting.

Over the next few days, I received new revelations from the Word of God. I had always been impatient, wanting to do things in my timing. I had demanded that my birthday be celebrated, that my parents send me to the convent, that they get me tutors. Through hard work and determination and sometimes sheer stubbornness, I had been able to overcome every obstacle in my path. But not with this cancer.

Psalm 5:3 tells me that the Lord hears my voice when I lay my requests before Him, waiting in expectation. Now that I was trusting God to fight the battle for me, I needed only to be still and watch what was happening. I didn't go over the scenarios in my mind, the what-ifs; I didn't harbor any anger. Fear was hard to overcome, but at this point, I felt I could truly live day-by-day, thanking and blessing the Lord.

The spiritual battles were the hardest of all. Physically I was drained, nearly dead, but with the help of the doctors and the grace of God, I was getting through it. The need to demand control, impatience, and doubt—the essence of fear—were like tumors on my soul, tumors that the chemotherapy of prayer could overcome. The problem was that unlike physical tumors, over which I had little control, these spiritual tumors could come back because I let them. Sometimes I invited them; sometimes they crept back, unnoticed until they had taken charge of my heart and mind. It was a daily battle for me to trust God and allow Him to fight this different sort of cancer.

My birthday, which was on September 27, came and went. The girls in the office posted a video on my blog wishing me well. How I wished I was back at work with them! But during this time, I was experiencing the infinite grace of God. I was weak from anemia, but I could get around the house and do personal things like take a bath and go to the bathroom. While I had lost weight, I was able to maintain what I had.

The weekend was even better because Zach came to visit. We also got the wonderful news that David and Alicia were expecting a baby on February 12!

Then I returned to the University of Chicago for more chemo along with a lumbar puncture. These treatments made me so tired. I hoped that I would feel much better soon and that I would live to see my grandchild.

CHAPTER 20: The Journey Onward

Clouding my joy was the knowledge that the family conflict that had flared up in the months after my diagnosis had not been resolved. How I prayed that God would restore peace to us all.

Dr. Stock had promised me that I could go back to work six months after the graft, and that is exactly what God allowed to happen. It was a happy day for me when she gave me the news. "Anjuli, you are cancer-free. You can go back to work and enjoy every minute of what you want to do."

"I want to invest in my staff, as they have invested in me," I told her.

"Then go and do what you enjoy doing most."

My cancer would not be behind me had my staff not been behind me. I never knew what loving, serving employees I had until I became sick. They were no longer employees, but family. This knowledge was a rose God plucked and handed to me along with the cancer.

I'm still not allowed to see patients, of course, because my T cells have not yet developed, meaning I have no immune system. All of the immunity I built up to tetanus, polio, bacteria—all was wiped out. Like a newborn child, I'm receiving inoculations against all of those diseases. But I can have the staff present patients to me, and I can advise on the treatment.

I am thrilled that I am still on this earth. Every day, every minute I am sustained by the grace of God and His mercy toward me. I did what I could in the scientific realm, but I had to really trust the Great Physician. I have personally experienced Who He is.

My story may be different from others, but this is the way the Great Physician got the attention of this minute atom. I have to say that because of He did get my attention, cancer is the best thing that has happened to me. I have learned that it's not about me; it's about the holy, sovereign God Whom we serve. So many good things have come out of this journey as I have had the time to dwell on His immeasurable love and grace. These were always there, but they are renewed for me. The Lord is teaching me to be a better wife. I thought I was the greatest wife before, but I never took the time to commune with my husband. It's so wonderful to be able to do that now.

In church I was taught that the proper order of priorities is God, family, and work. I thought I had them in order, but I found I did not. How can I have God as my first priority if I fill up my life with stuff? I was kind of using Him. He was always there for me, but I only picked Him up when I needed Him, the way I could pick up the little statues of Hindu gods. That's not the way we should live. God convicted me of that.

Sometime during the fall, I had my third vision of God. I was sleeping in the condo we'd bought in Burr Ridge, a suburb of Chicago. Since we realized I'd need to be monitored frequently over the next months and years, it made sense to us to buy a place that would be more convenient for getting to the University of Chicago than from our home in Bloomington.

Around three in the morning, I woke up to see Jesus standing in my room. He was wearing a beautiful robe and had a humble face. He was holding out His hands to me, saying, "Come to me all who are heavy laden, and I will give you rest." I was so excited to see Him, but before I could respond, He disappeared. Rest was something I prayed for daily. He offered it freely; I simply needed to let Him give it to me, rather than manufacture it on my own.

On October 26 I had my seventh bone marrow biopsy. Dr. Stock said I needed to continue the chemo. I was all right with that. My old fear was being replaced by faith, and I continued to live each day by the grace of God. My fear of losing control had disappeared. This cancer had truly been a divine appointment.

I'm feeling more and more the comfort of the Lord. I feel the healing of the Lord flowing through me. They say I have a chemo brain, one clouded by the effects of all the poisons they have pumped into me. It is true I have trouble remembering where I put my keys or what I was about to say, but I am able to focus. I can focus on the cross and see the nails that go into His hands. And when I think of the fear I have of my upcoming lumbar puncture, of the medications that will flow into my body, all those fears have totally disappeared. Why? Because the Lord is my Comforter. As long as we allow the Holy Spirit to comfort us, we can carry the cross He has given us to bear.

CHAPTER 20: The Journey Onward

I had another lumbar puncture with chemo on November 2. I reflected on the most important gift the cancer had given me, and that is time. I'd been able to reconnect with my husband and restore relationships in which I had never had the time to invest. I was more in tune with the needs of my body than I had ever been before. I was also grateful that the cancer had come when I had an empty nest and didn't have to be caring for the needs of my children.

God allowed this crisis of cancer to take me to a place to which He had never before taken me. There is a lot of pain involved, but nothing except extreme suffering would be able to do this work. I can now live in today, in now. I used to think I had unlimited time on this earth to do all I wanted to do. All I can do now is glorify God. As I rest and recover from the chemo, I rely on the Lord and the prayers of my friends and family.

Thanksgiving came and went, one when my family was doubly thankful. Eleven months earlier we did not think I would see the New Year, let alone survive through the summer and fall. Through the Internet, I was able to hear the orphans we support in India sing "Amazing Grace" and to share in their worship.

But this Thanksgiving was not without pain. Just after the holiday, David and Alicia broke from the family. The stress of this whole experience had ripped apart our family. The unresolved conflicts of the past few months had grown into festering sores that ate through the bonds between us. Since then, they have refused any contact with us. The agony of this rupture, on top of the emotional toll of the cancer, was almost more than I could bear. God would have to help me through this trial, for I could not overcome it on my own.

Once again I turned to Dr. Tobin for support. We'd been meeting weekly and had made great progress in managing the anxiety and depression that came with my cancer, but this event was the most heartbreaking emotional trauma a mother could experience. I was very attached to David, as he was my oldest son. I had inspired him to become not just a doctor, but an allergist, and we'd talked about his taking over my practice.

Dr. Tobin, being a mother, understood my pain and was not only sympathetic but inspired me to come up with methods to handle the situation. I admired her for her mode of counseling as she always encouraged me to find a solution. In a later visit, she would ask if it was working and would congratulate me for finding the light in a dark tunnel. I would always express great thanks for her help. She would always respond, "Dr. Nayak, you figured this out for yourself."

Soon after Thanksgiving, I had to discontinue my chemotherapy because of some problems with my blood counts. On November 30 I returned to the University of Chicago to discuss my options and which chemo I would be taking. I still believed that I was healed. No matter how much I wanted to crumble, I refused to give into tears and fears. It was not easy for me to trust the Lord all of this time, but I was learning more and more Who the Great Physician was.

With all we had been through as a family and a community, I realized how important it was for all of us to pour out ourselves in prayer for each other. I also had to count my blessings every day. Yes, I had a bad disease, but God was restoring me for His glory. This faith gave me hope. Sometimes things didn't go the way I wanted them to, but I reminded myself that they would all pass away. Sometimes I woke up in the morning and thought the cancer was simply a bad dream. Then I realized it was the reality of my life now—the life God had given me.

On December 8, I received a gift from my office staff: a large album with greetings and photos. What a blessing to read their encouraging and loving notes. The gift made me think of why I went into medicine in the first place: I wanted to be a healer. For many years, I was. Now I'd had an encounter with the greatest Healer of them all.

I continued to be on chemo, and I faced the reality that I might be on it for the rest of my life. The Great Physician would sustain me, whatever came. I had learned to spend time with God like Mary did, to let the hustle and bustle fade from my life. When I did, the peace of the Lord that passed all understanding filled my heart and my mind.

Despite the absence of David and Alicia, we had a joyful Christmas—Nick, Zach, Luke, and I. My spirits were up, and I felt good. When I was

CHAPTER 20: The Journey Onward

diagnosed, we didn't think I would make it to Christmas. And here I was, having had not one but two more Christmases with my family. I realized that life is all about love—love that is unconditional.

January 17, Zach accompanied me to my appointment with Dr. Stock. We sat in the exam room, wondering what news the day would bring. We'd had so many setbacks and never knew what to expect.

Dr. Stock came into the room and announced, "All your blood tests, all your counts are negative."

I sat, stunned. I had never expected to hear her say these words. Zach was staring at Dr. Stock with wide eyes and his mouth hanging open. We both held our breath, waiting for her next statement. "Anjuli, your graft is working. You have new blood cells that are not cancerous. After this long battle, one that's lasted more than a year, I congratulate you."

I could feel the hair on my arms rise up. Joy overflowed in my heart. After Zach and I left Dr. Stock, we sat in the waiting room and sang songs of thanks and praise to God.

Soon after that appointment, I recorded the following for my blog:

Why God has chosen to heal me and not others, I cannot answer. Perhaps He saw great need, or great faith, or was moved by compassion. I have no clue. I can only give praise and glory and honor and thanksgiving to Him. At times I have gone through the valley of the shadow of death, but at all times He has comforted me.

There were times I could have lost hope, but my hope rests in the power of His resurrection and His promises. I pray that now I can be an effective servant for Him, to be His eyes, hands, and feet, and that my testimony will touch the hearts of people and lead them to the cross.

It is an awesome privilege to be alive. The Great Physician is not done with me. He has plans for me that are greater than mine. He is reforming me and restructuring me in each cell of my body so I can be an effective servant. The process is still on. Every day I have down moments, but He walks with me.

Every day is a brand-new day, and all I can do is surrender to Him. Surrender is something that was so difficult for me. From the time I became a Christian, I always prayed and worshiped and read the Word of God. But did I ever surrender to Him completely? Very few times in my life. I am now learning to do this every day.

Today, I am healthy and smiling, and I have more strength. But I still have not been able to return fully to work. I am not allowed to see patients yet. Hopefully in the spring, that will happen. I pray that God gives me a direction for how God wants to use me for His kingdom. I also am excited about being a grandma, when David and Alicia's baby is born. I pray that we can reconcile so I can see the baby.

In February I gave my testimony at a women's retreat. I shared:

I stayed in the hospital on multiple occasions over the next nine months. The Lord appeared to me three times. I kept a journal every day. I don't recall a major part of my treatment. All I recall is a large clock on the wall ticking away, day after day, night after night, as I was unable to sleep. I was preparing myself to die, never expecting to come home and live. I was ridden with fear, terror, discouragement, despondency, and self-pity. In a state of shock, I realized that during all of my years in medicine, I had witnessed miracles, and there is a Healer Who performs them. Trust me, I have experienced Him. Today, I have been impacted by His healing! My cancer is gone, and the Philadelphia chromosome, which caused it, is no longer detected in me. Who, except the Great Physician, has the knowledge and wisdom to explain this?

God hates everything that causes us pain, but great works are done in deep pain. In all of this, we have come to know God, His Son, and His Spirit in ways we have never before experienced. Jesus heals and continues to do so. No one has ever said that it would be easy in the midst of storms, but He is the Comforter and the blessed Controller of all things. He is the same, yesterday, today, and tomorrow. He knows the big picture He has in mind for my life.

I think of my cancer as a rebirth. Cancer stripped me of my pride, arrogance, earthly pleasures, and degrees. Cancer made me humble. Cancer gave me time to sit at the Lord's feet for long periods of time that I did not have or spare before. Cancer ruptured my sins of disobedience and disrespect to my husband. I was loud, abrasive, and always wanting to be a winner, especially when it came to arguments. My three sons have

CHAPTER 20: The Journey Onward

been greatly affected by cancer also. Almost a year after my diagnosis, David and his wife walked out of our lives. There is no communication from them to us. This is an emotional cancer that I grieve every day of my life. I urge you all to pray that I would get a glimpse of my firstborn grandchild, due in one week.

It has become obvious to me that cancer is not my greatest enemy. My greatest foe is anything that keeps me from living in intimacy with the Lord. Unbelief, lack of trust, self-sufficiency, unsurrendered fears, self-centered habits and patterns of thinking are a few of the things God wanted me to address. Cancer was simply the tool He used to cause me to stop and listen to Him—to really listen to Him. In that sense, cancer was an incredible blessing from God. There is no rest without surrender. We don't doubt that God has His best in store for us; we wonder how painful His best might be. This is exactly where I am. I am convinced all of this is for my best. But I wonder how much more pain I will have to endure.

I don't know how much longer I have to live, but in reality, neither do you. I'll plead with you: if you've never put your hope in God, don't wait another day! Life is too short to waste on cheap thrills, nice stuff, and meaningless accomplishments. I can honestly say that I have never had so much joy as I have had since being diagnosed with cancer. All that is meaningless has been stripped away. Loving God and loving people have become paramount. Life is drastically different, but it has never been so good.

Chapter 21

Surviving and Thriving

I was blessed to be able to share that testimony at the women's retreat, as I truly wanted to be used by God in some way. Often I feel like a baby in a test tube, whom God is remaking and reshaping through the Holy Spirit. I feel I am a better person than I was before the cancer, a better vessel to be used by God. I have never forgotten the angel who told me I was being given another chance. I want to take full advantage of that chance.

As I continued to heal, the Lord inspired me to reach out to others. I made efforts to start a cancer support group and reach out to Indian women in the community. I wanted to use the time He gave me in service to Him and to others.

Still there were challenges. My immune system was still like that of a newborn's, as the immunizations I was given did not take, we had to repeat the shots. It was in God's timing, not mine, that my immune system would return to normal. I knew the Enemy was already defeated. He threw darts at me that made me feel fearful and anxious. But by an act of my will, I would follow Jesus wherever I was alive, whether in this earth or in heaven.

March 12, 2012, was my "first birthday," the one-year anniversary of my transplant. Who would have thought I would be alive this long? My

CHAPTER 21: Surviving and Thriving

one-year bone marrow biopsy was done, and the results were testimony to God's power. I was totally free of cancer! Who but the Great Physician could do a job like this? I had been taking thirty-four pills a day; by my birthday, I was down to one.

I thought back to the three times the Lord had appeared to me during this journey. The bottom line was that it was all about faith. I learned that daily I had to ask God to diminish my doubts and increase my faith. What good is my faith if I turn my troubles over to Him and then continue to worry about them? There were holes in my heart, but God worked in all my circumstances. Many of the areas of my life that had been dark were opened up and addressed.

Mother's Day came, and with it some wonderful news. My immune system was finally working again, and I had immunity against various diseases. I had been healed. This was a total miracle of God, and I could not take the smile off my face. I could finally kiss my dog. I had been to the gates of Hades, and God had rescued me. I may be here today and gone tomorrow, but I will still give thanks to God.

However, it seems with every bit of good news, there was a setback. Soon after receiving the news of being cancer-free, I was diagnosed with pneumonia. Nick seemed so weary and burdened already, and this news didn't help.

By the end of May I was back out of the hospital. Along with the pneumonia, I had a little fender bender with my foot and ended up with a broken toe.

Each day, when I focused on eternal things, the things of the Lord, I could feel His love, joy, and peace. When I focused on myself or the way I used to plan or do things, I got a feeling of turmoil. My primary goal now was to invest my life in the lives of those around me and to live in a spirit of thankfulness for every day that had been given to me. I asked the Lord to increase my faith, which helped me keep from getting caught up in thinking in circles of what-ifs. God knew the answers.

Around the start of May, I started to realize that I went to see Dr. Stock every other week and talked to her for fifteen or twenty minutes, and I spent much of the time between appointments, wondering what the next test would show or what news the next consultation would bring. What was I supposed to do in the meantime?

For several months I'd been struggling mentally and spiritually. After my return home, I'd begun to lose my way. Confusion and questions about connecting with God had flooded my mind, and empty darkness loomed over me. I was like a performer in the circus, flying off one trapeze but not quite making it to the next. Weak, unsure, and vulnerable, depression and despondency overcame me. I was desperate for a new beginning.

God started teaching me that the best moment is right now. I was eager to do things now—rather than simply waiting and worrying. So I started searching for the best way to deal with my life as it was in the day I was in. I looked online and talked to people who had dealt with cancer, whether as patients or as a family member of someone who'd had the disease.

I also thought about my state of health. My body was weak; my muscles lacked any tone or power. My arms and legs tingled, and I had bouts of diarrhea and reflux. I was moody and had difficulty concentrating or sustaining a chain of thought. For the past nine months I'd had a physical therapist come to my home twice a week to work with me. I had also recruited a yoga teacher to come to my home as well. *Surely there is more I can do.*

Between the results I'd seen from the physical therapy and yoga, as well as my own research and experimentation, I started to put things together. The doctors only treated me medically. They did a heroic job in beating back my cancer, giving me back my life. But that was all they could treat. My battered body needed to be built back up, and I needed to adjust to the life I had been given, one that would never be the same as the one I'd had before my cancer diagnosis.

My first step was to start going for additional physical therapy. Previously, due to my lack of immune system, I'd had to have home therapy, but now I'd progressed to the point that I could be out among people.

At the physical therapy center, the therapists worked on my muscles and gave me so much more. They introduced me to the concept of cancer

CHAPTER 21: Surviving and Thriving

survivorship, the idea that cancer survivors need to take an active role in adjusting various areas of their lives in order to have a higher quality of life. They recommended several books pertaining to areas of survivorship and holistic living that would help me in my journey.

I ordered all of those books and voraciously read each one of them. Most of them pertained to survivorship of breast cancer, but so much applied to my own situation. One thing was clear: if I wanted to live well, happy, and healthy, I needed an integrated approach for all parts of my life: spiritual, mental, physical, and emotional. If I spent my time bringing a cohesive approach to all these areas of my life, my journey would be a lot more bearable. This plan resonated with me. I could see how this idea of survivorship could provide the solution for my struggles with anxiety and depression.

So I got to work. As a cancer survivor, I needed to address the medical, physical, nutritional, emotional, spiritual, and vocational issues created by my cancer. I thought about each area in turn, and I came up with plans for addressing it. In this way I developed my own survivorship plan.

Medical issues were well taken care of by Dr. Stock and the others at the University of Chicago Hospital. But when I thought about physical fitness, I realized how much ground I had lost due to the effects of the chemo. Through physical therapy, I started to regain muscle mass and strength. Over time, I developed an exercise plan to keep working toward developing strength and stamina.

Then I thought about nutrition. My digestive tract was still very fragile, not having completely recovered from being burnt out by the chemo. I didn't have the enzymes I needed for proper digestion, so I suffered from heartburn, bloating, and diarrhea. Consulting with a nutritionist helped me learn some healthier ways of cooking and which foods my system could tolerate more easily. Much of what they taught was knowledge I had learned during my practice of medicine but hadn't paid much attention to. Now I understood what a mistake that was, and how important good nutrition is.

Turning my thoughts to my emotional needs, I realized how crucial my weekly meetings with Dr. Tobin had been. Cancer survivorship is not simply physical healing, but establishing a new "normal" and loving it. Without her and her support, I don't think I would have been able to climb out of the deep pit in which I found myself. I committed to continuing at least monthly sessions with her, to make sure I continued to manage the intense emotions I battled through the ups and downs of my recovery.

Then came the vocational questions. As fervently as I wanted to return to work, I had to accept that it would not be possible. I simply didn't have the stamina to keep up with my practice, and for me, it was an all-or-nothing proposition. I didn't want to try to work part-time, or not to keep up with the latest research in immunology. Once I accepted this painful reality, I began to search for some other way I could use my time and talents so that I wouldn't have to spend my days focused on my cancer.

In this way, God led me to take a sabbatical from my ministry of medicine and spend time with the practices of spiritual disciplines of retreat and rest. Through my reflections, I realized that my efforts at Bible study and prayer, even in the darkest days of my treatment, had been critical to my recovery. By clinging to God and His promises, I was better able to cope with facing my own mortality. This realization left me wanting more. I began striving to engage in prayer, meditation, fasting, and study. These choices led me to dialogue with God. Oh! How it warmed my heart! My desires for His presence and my spiritual longings became like a boat's sailing across endless oceans, never in search of a harbor or an anchor.

I knew that all of these areas had to be connected deeper together in my soul and spirit, and that this building this connection would not be an intellectual exercise. My life had to be lived from the inside out, not the outside in, as I had been living it prior to my cancer. The books also taught me that I had to completely shut off my false self, my ego, my materialistic attachments, and to live out of my true self.

I went to seminars and retreats to learn breathing exercises, relaxation, and centeredness with temperance. I also became disciplined and compliant about my yoga, as it developed an inner sense of peace

CHAPTER 21: Surviving and Thriving

and restoration, calmness and stability. I started to journal, writing each day what I was thankful for as I enjoyed the beauty of God in nature. What a change for someone whose entire life was all about achievement!

Writing a survivorship plan is something I wish I had known to do right after my transplant. The resources are available, and the doctors told me about some of them; I simply didn't know I needed to take the initiative to seek them out. I have continued to work on these issues, taking charge and ownership of my cancer and how I'll live my life as a survivor. Rebuilding my life is a full-time job, making me busier than I ever thought I could be.

At one point I talked with my doctors at the University of Chicago. I learned that pediatric patients get more guidance in the area of survivorship than adults. The doctors who treat adults barely have time to deal with all of the medical issues. While they do that well, at times working miracles, there is still a void for those who survive the initial treatment of the disease. Like many people, I didn't know the work that would need to be done to give me an enjoyable quality of life after the intense stages of medical treatment were completed.

At the end of June, I reflected that, at almost sixteen months post-transplant, I was actually starting to have confidence that I would make it, that I would truly beat the cancer. It's one thing to know this intellectually, but when this assurance penetrates your heart, peace and joy overflow.

In spite of needing to return to the hospital from time to time, my body is recovering slowly but steadily, and my energy is returning. It's been like climbing up a mountain. I'm sticking to my nutrition and exercise plans, and most of all, staying close to Jesus' feet. As a physician, I've realized there's not much in our control. We can know things with our intellect and apply them to our patients, but ultimately what will happen is what the Great Physician wants. So we have to submit our desires to Him.

Over the summer, my Epstein-Barr titers started swinging up and down. When they were very high, my mind swirled, agitated and tumbled like the clothes in a washing machine. I wondered if I had another cancer or if I would have problems with my lymph nodes or some other part of my body. I had to remind myself that the battle belongs to God, and I simply need to do what I am supposed to do.

Telling myself that and doing it were two different things. Even though my cancer is gone, I get frequent infections that last a long time and require double the normal time to recover. I am rarely able to knock out infections on my own. If I start off with a runny nose, it goes into my lungs, and I suffer with persistent coughing for weeks.

Epstein-Barr was a bit more worrying than other infections. Dr. Stock told me to wait and see. She didn't want to treat me for Epstein-Barr, which would have involved more chemo. Of course, that announcement caused fear. I decided not to give in to the what-ifs. If Dr. Stock wanted to repeat the test in three or four weeks, I wouldn't worry about it for four weeks. Perhaps nothing would happen. Most of our worries are because the Enemy occupies our minds. I took those thoughts captive and let God have victory over them.

Finally we got the news that my Epstein-Barr titers were back to normal. One more answer to prayer, one more hurdle surmounted.

But sometimes, with each passing day the hurdles get higher and more difficult to overcome. My GI tract is still so weak due to the burning of the chemo. I have problems digesting milk and soy products, and I can never come close to eating raw meats and fish. I miss my sushi dearly. My hair is thin, and I am balding. Accepting these changes in my life are like rungs on a ladder I have to climb daily. Some days I can bound up to the top rung; other days, simply putting my foot on the lowest one takes all of the emotional energy I can muster.

Yet another setback came in the form of shingles, which appeared across my back and side two days after my birthday. By the end of October they were much better, and I was able to look forward to Zach's wedding in November. When I was diagnosed with cancer, I did not know how many milestones in my children's lives I'd be able to witness. But I was able to see Zach's medical school graduation a year and a half ago, and now I'll be able to participate in his wedding. It will be a day of great celebration.

CHAPTER 21: Surviving and Thriving

I have never asked God why He gave me cancer because I know that all things work together for good for those who trust in Him. I do not know what the ultimate purpose of my cancer was, but I had no choice but to accept it. So many times I cried out to the Lord, "Father, take this cup away from me," especially when I was in an immense amount of physical pain. But in the end, the prayer always had to be, "Not my will, but Yours, be done."

The New Year came, and I saw 2013 arrive, something that had seemed impossible when I was first diagnosed. I continued with my survivorship plan, exercising, growing stronger, feeling more confident about my future.

Soon after the New Year, I joined a spiritual transformational community. A few months earlier, a friend had told me about it, and I started reading the information on its website. I become interested because I wanted to seek God and know Him on a much deeper plane. I wanted to learn a more meaningful and deeper way of experiencing God.

By joining the community, I was able to learn to live a life with spiritual rhythms, which helps me experience God in a more personal way. Most significant to me were silence and solitude, contemplative prayer and care for the soul. All of these were new to me. In my life before cancer, I didn't have time for such pursuits or even know about them. Caught up in my drive to achieve, I probably wouldn't have seen much value in them. But these are the tools that lead me to experience the love of God in a deeper way, a love that is a well that never runs dry. This indeed is my true religion, where I belong to the greatest love of all. God is the Gardener Who prunes the thorns and brings out beautiful roses within me—roses that are filled with His aroma. I know now the identity of the Master Gardener of my first, earliest memories.

In the middle of May, my cancer was showing signs of returning to my bone marrow. Within a week, my body was subjected to chemotherapy yet again, and my mind and spirit to mental agony and thoughts of impending death. The situation seemed hopeless, with thoughts of a second transplant impossible to entertain. Every scenario before me was hard and gloomy.

My thoughts were unstable, flying all over due to high levels of prednisone. Images of being bald, having multiple intravenous lines, and staying in a hospital bed for six months upset me. Sometimes I woke up in the morning with my brain clouded with fear, anxiety, dread of the future. My mind flooded with questions. *What if my blood tests come back bad? What if I can't tolerate the chemo? What if I have a reaction? What if we never reconcile with David? Will I ever see my grandchild? What if I need a second transplant?*

Multiple procedures, including spinal taps and bone marrow biopsies, were done within a dizzying three weeks. I met with Dr. Stock, and the consultation did not end well. She gave me options: one was to start and continue chemotherapy for the next six months. The depression I experienced at the thought propelled me into silence and solitude. I stopped answering my cell phone and meditated in front of Jesus.

Thus I embarked on yet another journey, not knowing where it would lead me. This was a calling through the path of suffering and prayer, to be in touch with both ebb and flow, and to know Who God is. I had to make the decision to release the world and my fate into the hands of God. I was to act dependent on God and God alone. Psalm 46:10, "Be still, and know that I am God" became my mantra. I started to embrace silence and solitude and meditation, and how they brought me a deeper sense of God's presence.

The relapse of my ALL prompted a change in my chemotherapy regime. Dr. Stock told me that I would have to have a second transplant and that I would need to be on chemo for six months before that could be done. She was also looking at putting me on a new trial medication. The first two weeks after I received that news, I was depressed and anxious. I did not know if my life was going to end. Zach and Luke came over, and we held a family conference. I could not make any decisions, but they said they would support me all the way through. I was despondent. Christ was there, and He was my strength. He said, "Anjuli, be still and know that I am God. Be still, and be."

As I spent time in solitude and thought over the possibilities, I found that I was not afraid of dying because I know where my eternal

CHAPTER 21: Surviving and Thriving

home is. In my Father's home are many rooms, and I am going there. At this time my soul totally belonged to God, and my life was hanging by a thread. The chances of recovery after a second relapse are very slim. The survival rate is only 10 to 15 percent. Dr. Stock was very anxious, and so was I. In this, God embraced me, and I clung to Him like a child. There was so much calmness and harmony in that silence. In that crucible a voice was telling me, "I will go before you; you just be still. I will fight the battles for you."

Sometimes I woke up in the morning, my brain clouded with fear, anxiety, dread of the future. Finally, about the third week, the struggle stopped. I knew that God was going to be with me, above me, behind me, on my right and on my left, and in my very being through the Holy Spirit. In spending time in silence and solitude, Christ and me alone, the peace that passes all understanding filled my heart. Although the thoughts of a second transplant and the toxic effects of the chemo were in my mind, I conquered them because Christ was right there. As soon as those thoughts of suffering physically would come, I would replace them with a Scripture. And I thought that if God had brought me this far, He would take my journey to completion in His own time. Faith, which is able to believe the things we do not see, replaced my fear.

I realized the what-if questions came to mind when I thought of the future or the past. The past is gone; the future is unknown. I needed to think about the present and my relationship with God and to rest in Him. He would work in His way, in His timing, for His glory. I had to remember the promises of God.

I had a repeat bone marrow scan exactly one month after the first one that showed the return of my cancer. When Dr. Stock called me, she said, "Dr. Nayak, this is a miracle! I have never seen bone marrow as clean as this. You do not need any more chemotherapy. Don't even think of another transplant."

The bone marrow that had been filled with 75 percent cancer cells showed no cancer cells after one month. Some people could say it was the chemotherapy. But I had received that chemo before, and I could not tolerate it. I had severe headaches and could not even lift up my head.

But guess what? When it was restarted, I had no symptoms. Who was behind all this? God Almighty! He alone had the power to evaporate the cancer from my bone marrow.

That is exactly what happened in only four weeks. My heart is full of gratitude and thanksgiving. I can dwell in the peace that passes all understanding, which I could not do on my own. I am defeated when I try to do this on my own. Through the power of the Holy Spirit, I am blessed to live from the inside out. I do not have to seek an image of myself. I simply want to be in the presence of the Great I Am.

As time goes on, I keep trying to find God's plan for however long I have left. In September of 2013, I was accepted into the Master's of Spiritual Transformation program at the Northern Baptist Seminary in Chicago. I have learned that spiritual transformation is both natural and supernatural, and I want to learn more of the sacred rhythms that will set my heart and mind in expectation of what the Holy Spirit will do in my life. One of the disciplines I have learned is to meditate on five or six verses from the Scriptures, kneeling down, to allow the Spirit to work in me. One that means much to me is the one I heard Jesus Himself say, from Matthew: "Come to me, all you who are weary and burdened, and I will give you rest" (Matthew 11:28). I can feel the rest God gives me, even in my soul.

Between my coursework and keeping up with my survivorship plan, I have no time to brood, to feel sorry for myself, or to lapse into despondency. I have learned to be comfortable living in the cloud of the unknown.

Why did I get cancer? It wasn't sheer bad luck. It was God's redeeming plan for me. Why do some people survive a stem cell transplant and others don't? I have no clue. But I'm not supposed to know the answer to that question. All I know is that in the goodness of God I have been given a new life—not because of something I did or because I deserve it. God did this simply because He chose to do it. One thing of which I *am* sure is that this journey on earth will come to an end. For some, the journey is shorter than others, but at the end, we will have everlasting life. That new life will be so much more wonderful than this one.

CHAPTER 21: Surviving and Thriving

While I had cancer, I was totally stripped of all I had. I've learned so many truths and lessons through this journey. That God answers prayer. That we need to engage with others, praying for them and with them, allowing them to intercede for us. That I previously had a rote approach to prayer, simply considering it one item on my to-do list rather than a conversation with the One Who loves me and knows me better than anyone else. Learning to pray in this way is like maturing over a lifetime. It doesn't come in a day, but rather over time with much practice.

I have learned that I was lurching through life, following my own plans, oblivious to the fact that God had other, better plans for me. I never developed a clear vision for what His plans for me were. That while a busy schedule can result in a long list of accomplishments or a comfortable life, it's the time of quiet reflection spent with God that has the most significance, the place where my deepest needs are met.

While cancer was the catalyst for a rupture in our family, we don't yet know the end of that story. What we do enjoy are the stronger bonds between Nick, Zach, Luke, and me, the additions of Marcia and Rachel to our family, and the sweet reconciliation with my siblings.

When I was little girl in India wanting to be free, I never thought of the price I would pay to pluck myself from all I knew and the family that cared for me in order to graft myself into a foreign culture. Then I plucked myself from Hinduism to embrace Christianity. Then I was plucked out of my comfortable existence to go on a journey with God that took me close to death and into greater intimacy with my children, husband, and God than I ever thought possible. Cancer taught me I had to go down before I could go up. Looking back, I can truly say that while being plucked was painful, the process bore much good fruit in my life.

Through my suffering, I learned the truth that God yearns for me. His desire is so great that He wrote my name into the palm of His hand. In Hindi, *Anjuli* means "an offering to the Almighty." That's what I am learning to be—a living offering to the One Who loved me and gave Himself for me.

To God be the glory for ever and ever. May we all know how high and wide and deep and broad is the love Christ Jesus has for us, for I am living proof that His love is bigger than any enemy which comes against us.

A Note from the Author

My hope is that this book has been inspirational and useful to you. If my story has helpful you in any way, then I can feel that my battle with cancer has benefited others.

While the word "cancer" does denote a certain set of universally shared and painful set of experiences, not all types of cancer are the same. In fact, cancer within the same organ sharing the same staging may not be the same experience for each patient. Conferring with your team of doctors will provide the best treatment plan for you and your family.

In gratitude for the care I received at the University of Chicago Medicine, all royalties from the sale of this book will be donated to the University of Chicago Cancer Research Foundation, to enhance cancer care, develop more effective and safer therapies, and promote prevention and screening research. If you would like to join me in supporting the University of Chicago's life-saving cancer research, please send a check to The UCCRF, 5841 S. Maryland Avenue, MC1140, Chicago, IL 60637 or visit http://cancer.uchicago.edu/help/donate.shtml.

www.ingramcontent.com/pod-product-compliance
Lightning Source LLC
Chambersburg PA
CBHW031415290426
44110CB00011B/396